Just Because
Your Kids Drive You
Insane...
Doesn't Mean You Are A
Bad Parent!

Just Because
Your Kids Drive You
Insane...

Lisa Barker

Doesn't Mean You Are A
Bad Parent!

www.lulu.com

www.lulu.com

JUST BECAUSE YOUR KIDS DRIVE YOU INSANE...
DOESN'T MEAN YOU ARE A BAD PARENT!

For information, address Martin Ola Press / Parent To Parent

editor@parenttoparent.com

Or please write to Lisa Barker, P.O. Box 217, Greenfield, CA 93927

LisaBarker@jellymom.com

www.JellyMom.com

Cover art courtesy of www.hasslefreeclipart.com.

For

My Husband

&

My Children

You make me smile and laugh everyday.

Thanks be to God.

Contents

And Go...Tell Me Where it Went! *Weight Games *Exercising With Toddlers *Exercise? Me? *Five Pounds of Chocolate Converts To...What!?! *Momma Cow *Burn Fat At Night *Strong Like A Woman

Introduction

Parenting IS Insanity

Whether you choose to spend your days at home focused on homemaking and raising children, opt to stay at work to help financially support the family and go after additional vocational dreams, or strive to meet what might be called the most insane ideal of all—working from home—the one thing most parents should be able to agree on is that parenting IS insanity.

Little by little, the half-size and pint-size human beings wear us down simply by being themselves. And although I have met a few parents through my syndicated parenting humor column, Jelly Mom™, that seem to characterize the 'humorous venting' of these situations as proof that those who 'complain' are unfit, 'ignant' and 'unedumacated,' most are greatly relieved and appreciative to read that another parent shares the same frustrations, puzzlements and predicaments that they have. Casting these common themes in a humorous light also greatly decreases stress, renews our purpose and helps us to be better parents.

So I offer you this slim sampler of the best of Jelly Mom™, a humor column I write that is currently a regular feature in the Eureka (California) Reporter and on dozens of parenting and humor websites.

Whether you chase after toddlers all day, mix it up with middle-school-age children or have teens and fondly look back on their younger years, it's my hope that you get a good belly laugh out of my plight as a parent.

Best regards,
Lisa Barker

All proceeds from the sale of this book will benefit the Hugs and Hope Club. Created by Marsha Jordan in 2000, Hugs and Hope seeks to bring smiles to critically ill children and their families. For more information, please visit www.HUGSandHOPE.org.

They Never Told Me

I consider myself an older and wiser parent because I am no longer a 'newbie' still getting sucked in by marketing that claims I need a Diaper Genie and a butt-wipe warmer to be a good mommy.

Therefore, I feel qualified to look back on those early days of parenting and draw up a checklist of things they didn't tell me when I signed up for the Parent Corps.

12. No one ever told me that I'd learn to dive like an Olympic distance swimmer every time my little ones reached for an electrical outlet.

11. No one ever told me that I'd lie and tell my kids it isn't pepper, it's a secret ingredient that LOOKS like pepper, but isn't, and that it tastes really good.

10. No one told me it would take just one week to potty train my twins and eight YEARS to get my boy to stop wetting the bed.

9. No one told me that for every child I'd had, I'd adopt at least two more from the neighborhood. Where do these kids keep coming from? They can't all be mine!

8. No one ever told me that popsicles and cookies were kid magnets and that every time I'd open my front door to treat my kiddos there would be a line forming that went around the block.

7. No one ever told me that it would cost ten dollars an hour for somebody to watch the kids so I could park my car three streets over and enjoy a bit of peace.

6. No one ever told me that the mother who restricted sodas, candy and sugar cereal when I was growing up would buy these very same things in jumbo quantities for her grandchildren.

5. No one ever told me that the silence I prayed for would be the very thing to keep me up all night nursing a sick kiddo back to health, just to hear the noise again.

4. No one ever told me that I'd turn into a miser, hiding secret stashes

of chocolate and treats around the house so there would be something left for me after the kids went through the cupboards.

3. No one ever told me how much fun it would be to disagree with the teacher or principal simply because I can now that I'm an adult.

2. No one ever told me that the kids would one day outgrow the imaginative and make-believe aspects of holidays like Halloween, Christmas, Valentine's Day and St. Patrick's Day, but I wouldn't.

1. No one ever told me that parenting would be the toughest job I'd ever love.

Just Because

Your Kids Drive You

Insane…

Doesn't Mean You Are A

Bad Parent!

Chapter One

~Toddlers~

The Daily Unraveling of Sanity

Good-bye Mattel & Company

Dear Mattel and Company,

Our Momma is going to give away all our toys. She means it. We don't care a whit about all the cars, blocks, stuffed animals and battery operated noisemakers that we have. So Momma is giving them all away to charity and leaving only our favorite playthings around the house.

Things like:

Clean laundry. We love to strew it all over the floor and roll in it before Momma can fold it.

The television remote. This is so much more fun than any noisemaker because it changes the channel and makes Daddy make noise!

Momma's glass of orange juice. Whee! The itsy bitsy spider went up the garden wall. Down came the OJ and washed the spider down.

The com*put3r k3yb0ar/d. It+s su/ch gr3at fu/n t0 h3lp m0mma typ3!

Dog food. Not only does dog food kibble instantly cover the maximum square footage of floor space, it's fun to watch Momma fall on her behind as she comes running.

Sofa cushions. How inconvenient to have them tucked in properly. They are much more fun on the floor where we can hop from one to the other like frogs.

Throw rugs. There's nothing like dragging each other through the house on Momma's carefully placed throw rugs.

Pencils and crayons. The doors in our house used to be such a boring plain old white. Now they are much more colorful!

The mouse pad. Who's ingenious idea was it to make such a fun and floppy Frisbee?

Toilet paper. Oh, the uses are endless! We are so good at grabbing the end and running through the house weaving a delicate pattern around the furniture.

It's MUCH more fun to dump laundry detergent up and down the hall than it is to ride a tricycle.

It's much more fun to flush items down the toilet than it is to put blocks in a talking container.

It's so much more fun to mash banana on the laminate

floor and slip around than to roller skate.

Thanks for all the time you have taken to research our age group and scientifically define our developmental stages and TRY to invent toys that will please and delight and even educate. But we have learned so much about gravity simply by dropping our food all over the floor. We have learned to count by watching Momma's red face as she counts to ten. We already know how to do buttons, zippers and ties as we undress ourselves at least three times a day.

Now we need to close this letter and get busy taking all the folded sheets and towels out of the linen closet. SOMEBODY keeps folding them and putting them back. Our work is never done!

Best regards,
Becca (age 3) and Aiden (age 2)

The Great And Naked Houdini
& His Assistant

I followed the trail of clothing down the hall. Somehow, my two-year old son had freed himself from these repressive articles.

There were the pink jammy bottoms (hey, it's MY son and he's secure in his masculinity so he can endure this hand-me-down), then the t-shirt...and the diaper?

Nope. Hadn't gotten to that yet.

How does he DO that? The boy can't get a fork to his mouth, but he can strip and climb the highest bed, sofa or table with amazing ease.

I'm thinking his three-year old sister is an accomplice, especially since she's a self-styled nudist herself.

Why do toddlers do that? It's cute and sometimes annoying, but at the drop of a hat you see them streak through the house. Whee, no clothes!!

It was always a game when my eldest were toddlers. Fresh from the bath, and sometimes still dripping, round and round the house they'd race, chanting "Noodie doodie, noodie doodie!"

And you've got to be fast, too. Sometimes the thrill of streaking is a bit overwhelming and, well, there are accidents. Mind you, these are the un-potty-trained.

On the other hand, as much as the little ones enjoy their clothing emancipation, they've got a blankie the size of a queen-size bed throw. And here comes the three-year old now, thumb in mouth, giant pink-gray frazzled blankie in tow.

I recall using duct tape on my third child when he was in diapers. You know, duct tape, the ever-all-purposeful handy tool of veteran moms. If you've got duct tape, you can solve any problem. Ergo, the son with the gray 'belt' on his diapers.

(Duct tape, by the way, also keeps your television cabinet shut so one doesn't discover fistfuls of Cheerios and crayons in the VCR. Duct tape also helps brothers and sisters bond. When you've got bickering siblings and you threaten to make them conjoined twins for the rest of the day, they suddenly find it within themselves to practice a little charity with one another.)

But I digress.

The greatest feat of the knee-high bumpkins is their ability to open every single door you have carefully toddler proofed.

How is that an adult can spend twenty minutes trying to get into the bathroom and the two-year old can turn the knob in 15 seconds flat? Why does it take me a bit of effort to open a bottle of aspirin and a child no trouble at all? And what about those car seats?

Whoever thought that a nimble-fingered toddler COULDN'T slip the straps off her shoulders and wiggle her way out of the armrest must never have been a parent.

Hmmmmm. I'll have to remember to take her along the next time I go shopping. Just in case I leave my keys in the car.

Climb Every Mountain

I have this two-year old son who would climb Mt. Everest if it were in my living room.

The problem is he's afraid of heights.

That's right, anything over two-feet off the ground and he turns into Velcro Man.

So frequently I hear "Mummm, Mummm, Mummmma!" from some room in the house, and I can be sure to find Velcro Man clinging to the top of some dresser, counter, table, bookcase or bunk bed for dear life.

What does this say about my son?

No, he is not stupid. Moms do not like to consider that. Stupidity in children somehow equates with a degree of low intelligence and incapability in parents. If my son is stupid, I'm an unfit mother. It doesn't have to make sense. That's how moms think.

Instead, I think: My son readily and enthusiastically continues doing that which scares him the most. He's a risk taker. But he's cautious. Maybe he'll be a firefighter or a policeman. *Yeah...*

"Mummmmma!!" His cries break into my daydream.

I come running. He grins at me with his rodent teeth (you know how hamsters have those two long teeth on the bottom—that's my boy!) and who can resist such a grin? I can't.

I peel Velcro Man off his latest peak of glory and he cuts off the air to my lungs with his steel-armed grip around my neck. No, the boy was never dropped as a baby. He just doesn't like heights.

I set him down and he goes right back to his 'mountain' of choice and starts climbing. The higher he goes, the stiffer he gets, until at last, as if some unseen force freezes and immobilizes his muscles, he reaches for the top and cries, "MUMMMMMA!!!"

This is the boy we don't bother to strap into the highchair. He's a real cling-on.

In fact, if I want to keep him out of mischief I can just put him on a counter where he will remain sitting stiffly as if one itsy-bitsy move will set off an atom bomb. (Kidding.)

(I have to write 'kidding' in some of these columns. You never know when some childless-somebody is going to come by and take everything I write literally. It's up to the reader to discern fact from fiction, but some need a little help. I'm writing for pure entertainment, you know.)

Love Hurts

This is the second child I've had who has confused kissing with biting. Thanks to that confusion, I've got a nice array of bruises on my legs.

It's really something when you are dusting off the top of the refrigerator and along comes a pint-sized munchkin all ready to love you up unawares.

"OUCH! No, don't bite, that HURTS Momma!"

(Big rodent grin.) Who can stay mad at a face like that? Soon I return to my daily housecleaning.

Along comes Jaws.

"OUCH!! No, no, no!"

(The pitiful look of rejection.)

I pick my baby up and show him how to give 'kissies.'

Teaching a toddler how to kiss has, for me, anyway, been a bit like the randomness of a high school science experiment.

With one child you get bites. With another you get licked. With still another you get an open mouth pressed against you. And with yet one more you get a slap and a laugh.

I'm not going to contemplate what those responses translate into as far as the future development of my children's personalities go. I'd like to think that all my children will grow up to be warm, lovable people...as if they're not people now!

Well, they aren't—especially, my two-year old. Maybe we should start calling him 'Piranha.'

It takes a few months and several bruises to get kissing down. It takes a lot of fast footwork and even some football maneuvers to sidestep the onslaught of love bites.

But in the end, you get a toddler so pleased because she can share the greatest human emotion with her family. Then at every turn you're getting real kisses, butterfly kisses, kisses soft like an angel's.

But until that time, short of rubbing Tabasco sauce on your legs, you've got to love and dodge, love and dodge.

Now THAT'S the secret as to how moms lose weight when the kids reach the toddler years!

And you thought the new slim mom figure came from chasing the tiny tots. Nope, it comes from running for your life! OUCH!

The Meaning of No And Other Worthless Commands That Toddlers Ignore

I don't know about you, but in my house "No!" does NOT mean, "stop," "decease," "desist," "anti-go." My toddlers just don't get it. For that matter, every other parental command is meaningless as well. They all mean the same thing: Do the EXACT opposite…and do it as quickly as possible!

If one toddler is scaling the bookcase, "No!" doesn't mean "Get down," it means "Climb higher and faster!"

If the other toddler is taking books out of the same bookcase, "No!" means, "Dump as many books on the floor as you can before Momma catches up with you!"

If another toddler is crawling over the barrier to the area behind the television, "No!" means "Crawl faster and quickly pull out every cord as fast as you can!"

If still another toddler (I only have two but some days it feels like ten) has gotten into the cookies, "No!" and "Stop!" mean, "Quick, eat faster, *she's* coming!!"

And finally, when it's time to get dressed after a bath, "No!" means, "RUN, RUN, RUN!!! Sprint through the house before *she* can put clothes on you!"

Makes me feel a bit like Rodney Dangerfield. I get no respect!

It also makes me wonder what power a mom really has. My husband will walk into the room, see chaos and utter ONE command and all FIVE children STOP what they are doing! How is this possible?!

So I was contemplating all this the other day while I was literally half in the freezer, armed with a spoon and my sights set on the quart of chocolate ice cream. You know the moment. It's when the icy sweetness hits the back of your throat and "Ohhhhhhhhhhhhh, Heaven!"

Well, the toddlers sensed a disturbance in the Force. They KNEW that somewhere in the house I was experiencing some sense of peace and self-gratification. Obviously, it was because I wasn't standing over them saying, "No, no, no!" for the umpteenth time.

They soon spied my derriere sticking out of the freezer (we have a side-by-side).

"Hey, Momma, Momma!" They came running expectantly.

"Mnnnfph, mmmmph, nrfff, numphhhh!" I said, as I quickly gobbled as much ice cream as I could before they reached me! (Don't

14

tell me about the role reversal. Don't even suggest that I'm the one they get it from.)

"Cookie? Cookie?" They said, which is their catchall word for "Gimme something good and sweet to eat!"

"No," I said. No explanations and no breaking my heart with their pathetically cute expressions. Just big mean Momma saying "No."

And they got it! For the first time in a long time they understood the word "no." The spoon was now on the other foot!!

So I gobbled up a few more spoonfuls before they were on to me again.

And what is the moral of the story?

You expected one?

Then how about an oldie but a goodie: "Do as I say, not as I do!"

"Mnnnfph, mmmmph, nrfff, numphhhh!"

Toddler-proofing Your Home In
The New Millennium

My home looks like the typical baby-proofed home: guards on the electrical outlets, covers on the doorknobs, latches on the cupboards, and gates strategically set up to keep knee-high explorers safe. Which they don't! All they do is make life more challenging for the adults in the household.

These gadgets are outdated and no match for the baby of the new millennium. It only took two months before both toddlers understood how to get around these impediments to their curiosity. (Even the kittens know how to take out the little plastic pieces that plug into the outlet.)

Needless to say, the gates are all looking haggard and bent and they are pretty much useless due to little ones either running full speed into them to crash them down or wearing them down by scaling them.

The dilemma? How to keep the little ones out of rooms they don't belong in. The solution? Animatronics.

No kidding! I have one toddler that is scared to death of a dancing musical chicken I have (it clucks to the ever-popular 'Chicken Dance' song) and another that is TERRIFIED of the cute blue fuzzy monster made famous by Disney's "Monsters Inc."

So I have placed these motion sensory activated toys EXACTLY where I don't want the kids to tread. The results? SUCCESS!

I have both the pleasure of warding off children *and* hearing their screams so I know exactly where they are in the house. (In my childhood my mother and grandmother had eyes behind their backs. Now, as a parent, I have dancing toys that look possessed.)

"ROWWWWWWWRRRR!" says the blue monster. "EEEEEEEEEEEK!" says my two-year old.

"Get away from the computer!" I warn from the other side of the house.

"Pu-cock, PU-COCK!" pipes up the chicken. "Shrieeeeek!" screams my three-year old.

"Get out of the kitchen!" I call out from another room.

So I've stocked up on animated toys…and now my home looks like an exhibit at Disneyland. And the little ones sit quietly with unblinking eyes and severe facial tics…but let me point out that they are QUIET and not getting into everything.

And all this I do, not for some sense of retribution (to pay the little buggers back for constantly chipping away at my own sanity). Oh, no! No, not at all! No, siree, Bob! I'm doing this for their *safety*. Yeah, that's it.

Heaven knows I love these little ones and wouldn't want a thing to happen to them. Now pass me the remote...there's this talk show I want to catch while somewhere down the hall a chicken dances and a monster growls....

Justice and The Wee Ones

Even at 18-months, my youngest son knew when a horrible injustice has occurred. He, like all the rest of the children, came running to me with this look of utter self-righteousness. You know the look—it's the "How *could* she/he?????" look. Horror of horrors and sorrow of sorrows! Only mom can remedy the situation.

At least that's what they think.

The only justice there is when you have toddlers is injustice because all mom wants is a little peace and quiet.

"Give the ball back to Aiden," I say to my eight-year-old son.

"But, Mom, it's *my* ball."

The two-year old, still looking stricken and accusing, begins to dance in place while he cries for retribution.

"I don't care *whose* ball it is. Give it to him!"

The eight-year old complies and goes sulking to his room. The two-year old, completely satisfied, now sings praises to the ball and dances with it.

I sigh. What am I *supposed* to do? "He has things of mine, too, you know!"

It started way back when his older twin sisters were the age he is now. I lost several of the stuffed animals I'd saved from my childhood or that were given to me by my husband. At first I tried to get them back, but gave up because I was sure I'd go to hell for it—something about stealing from a baby—and two, after all the slobber from the toddlers they no longer looked like the fluffy little animals they used to be.

Slobber happens to be the way toddlers mark their territory. That's why anything in the house below an adult's waistline is considered the toddler zone. The table legs, the coffee table, the walls, the dog, all the toys, magazines and books are slimed because they are in the toddler zone, a.k.a. the slobber zone.

It's so gross that when my twins were three they asked if I would take their baby brother back to the hospital where I'd gotten him. He was worse than a Saint Bernard. But at least he didn't shed. And for entertainment he could burp on command.

So now the little caboose in our family is well on his way to expanding his vocabulary. This means that besides the Wail of Injustice he can tweak the rest of mom's nerves with cries of "Mine, mine, mine!" and "No, no, no!"

Once he starts one of his little mantras, I *have to* get up and go find out which child is trying to repossess his or her own toy.

"Just give it to him!"

The older child cries…the youngest child gives a sly sideways glance around the room coveting even more possessions.

Yep. He's got us all wrapped around his little finger all right. And he knows it. The only one he can't fool is dad, but I'm catching on.

He has this carefully practiced cry—perfected by trying it on his older sisters who cave in to his every demand because, yes, he's still cute as a button. Well, at the table, when he's told to behave, he'll break into crocodile tears. How do we know? He's got that sly sideways glance thing going, to see if we're falling for it.

"Faker!" we cry out and get a big rodent grin from him.

Well, at least he's being fair about it, or else I'd have to break out with the Wail of Injustice myself.

Forget Abu Ghraib, Use Toddlers

We don't need to keep people in these prison camps. We could sufficiently torture them and get them to spill all their top-secret information with just one stroller, two toddlers and three hours of running errands on foot.

Every Monday I hike a mile to the church, the post office, the bakery, back to the church again and then back home. This constitutes about three hours of my day. *Two and a half* of those hours involve my three-year old screaming at full volume while she hangs over the side of the stroller and slowly rotates her head 360 degrees while spitting pea soup.

For some reason this pleases her two-year old brother (seated in front of her) who begins to swing his head from side to side and sing. Whereupon, she sits up and repeatedly slaps him on the head, causing him to cry while she grunts out a hoarse "WAH! WAH! WAH!" with each hit.

By this time people on the streets are ducking into alleys and storefronts as I make my way through town. I'm so numb to the pain that I no longer see the stares or catch glimpses of those who frown and roll their eyes...I'm like Cujo. I'm far enough along in my insanity to know I'm sick and yet I don't want to hurt my family—I want to be put out of my misery as soon as possible...but this terrible urge is rising up inside me....

I now understand why some species eat their young.

What a small price to pay for some peace and quiet. What a great resource we have for national security! If only the powers that be would listen. I'd let them borrow my tots for the afternoon. Surely they could get to the bottom of most urgent matters in zero time with my toddlers in tow.

"Sir, we want to ask you a few questions."

"It depends on what you mean by the word 'questions'..."

"Okay, bring in the toddlers!"

"No! No, I'll speak! I'll do and say whatever you want!"

This is what my husband is like come Monday morning. Boy, is he ready for work! Give him one weekend with the toddlers and he can deal with any office politics you send his way—with a SMILE on his face.

I can inspire the same gratitude in my older children. Anytime they start bickering among themselves, I put them in charge of the toddlers. In less than half an hour I have 'tweens that are more than ready to be charitable with each other—anything to get away from the two tots.

Better yet, I can get through a checkout line in nothing flat if I take my cranky toddlers with me. Once they start up, people *MOVE* out of the way and the cashier does all she can to speed up the process. I get to go right to the front of the line at the post office.

This morning my husband was envying the fact that I get to sleep in two extra hours. I said, "Yes, but there's a trade off," I said, lifting my weary head and nodding toward the door. "THEM."

Down the hall, peacefully asleep yet, the toddlers were recharging their batteries for another day of torture for Mom.

So why are we wasting our tax dollars on anything but toddler power?

The Wonder of Children

When you have toddlers ordinary things become tools for extraordinary purposes. Take crayons for example. When I was a toddler I enjoyed dropping them down the heating vents where they would melt and ooze into a rainbow blob. I'm sure my mother really appreciated my artistic experimentation.

I don't, however, recall shoving them up my nose or in my ears as I have seen some of my children do.

Scribbles on the wall? That's the work of novices. But, eating crayons? Now were talking sophistication! There's nothing like a toddler with purple teeth.

Do you remember a craft from elementary school where you placed shavings from crayons between two pieces of wax paper that were then ironed together? It's the same premise as dropping crayons down the heating vents, but easier to preserve and a lot less messy.

Finger painting has to be the all time best activity there ever was to introduce to your children. It's funny to watch the expressions on your toddler's face as you *encourage* her to get messy. It's just as fun as showing them how to play in the mud.

The first time my twins did this (when they were toddlers) they wanted to wash their hands every three minutes—this from the kids that dreaded mom cleaning them with a washcloth. Soon, though, they were creating endless mud pies with great enthusiasm.

Now I have two more toddlers (ages three and two). My three-year-old is mentally at the same level as her younger brother, if not a bit behind. So it is much like having twins all over again. It's wonderful to walk with them and discover every sidewalk crack, every bug, feather, leaf, rock and scoop of sand. Everything must be touched (with fingers and toes), smelled, and tasted.

But every toddler is different. One wants to explore electrical outlets while another finds microscopic crumbs in the carpet. One wants to take apart everything he can get his hands on while another wants to fit every block into a small box.

It's the wonder they have for everything that draws parents to their hands and knees…and turns us into adult-sized pre-schoolers. *THIS* is why we end up speaking in the third person sounding like Elmo, or dancing like The Wiggles, or set out to explore the world like Dora.

Sometimes parents are chagrined to find they cannot switch

gears when they are FINALLY in the presence of other adults. I say, don't worry too much about it. You only have a few years to melt crayons, squish mud and poke about the world with your little ones. Live it up.

The Tale of The Skeenky Hepper

It starts with an odor that you and your spouse try to ignore. Then, you one-up each other with casual remarks about what that smell could possibly be. Finally, one of you dares to identify the stink HOPING that your spouse will own up to the fact that it's HIS/HER turn to attend to it.

When that doesn't happen, you make yourself get up and, supplied with the appropriate arsenal, you hunt down the malodorous perpetrator. There, in his bedroom, with his diaper completely off is your two-year old who apparently hasn't mastered the fine art of changing his own diaper. It's everywhere. "Skeenky!" he tells you. "Skeenky hepper!"

We have two kinds of "skeenky heppers" in our house. One lies around the house all day and only shows signs of life when I open a can

28

of dog food and plop it in his bowl. That would be our dog Pepper, whom my son calls "Hepper" and he is indeed "skeenky."

The other "skeenky hepper" happens to be just what you thought it was: a full diaper.

Nothing else on earth makes adults regress as rapidly as a "skeenky hepper."

"It's YOUR turn to change it!"

"No way, I did it last time. It's YOUR turn!"

"Is not!"

"Is too!"

Parents, just what type of behavior are we modeling for our children? Remember what all the parenting guides said? Children learn by watching us.

My husband gags and fans his face and makes a big production. "Ew, yuck, it's everywhere!"

"Well, hand me some wet paper towels...and a gas mask!"

He hands them to me on the end of a swimming pole, while pinching his nose.

Is this why the older children who are perfectly capable of changing their younger brother's diaper suddenly disappear whenever that odor, like a fine mist, slowly fills our home?

It's about the only time the kids behave absolutely perfectly...so as not to draw any attention to themselves.

"Here, take this outside to the garbage."

My husband runs like he has a hot coal in his hands. Kids

scatter. I reach for the air freshener. Now there really is a thick fog in our house. Little by little family members begin to return. At first they sniff cautiously, then take deeper breaths and soon the house returns to a normal level of chaos…until the *next* time.

The phone rings. It's my husband calling me with his cell phone from the car parked around the block. "Honey, I think the baby needs his pants changed."

I look outside and neighbors have roped off our house like a crime scene. A volunteer from the fire department stands in the middle of the street with a bullhorn. "Put the child down and back away slowly."

A helicopter circles overhead. They're getting ready to sanitize and deodorize. I've got seconds to make it out of the house. I run down the hall and out to the garage. The door is closing. I drop and roll, reaching back to grab my hat at the last moment before the garage door slams down. A swat team rushes the house and tense minutes later they emerge…with a sparkling baby boy held triumphantly in upraised arms.

When you have children in diapers, there's never a dull moment. In fact, I wonder why they haven't done a reality show featuring toddlers. Whether it's modeled after "Survivor" or "Last Comic Standing" (in this case, "Last Parent Standing") it certainly would be a captivating show.

Welcome To The Television Zone

The toddlers are watching too much television. So I am limiting their viewing now to just a few shows each morning. Naturally, they are having withdrawal. Oh, the tears and the protests!

The two-year old is hopping up and down. "Down, down, down!" he cries. Down with this idea, Mom!

The three-year old, a self-styled technician, keeps turning the television on and off, but all she can get is the music station I have it tuned to.

Worse, they know we have the SpongeBob movie and that's all they chant: "SpongeBob movie, SpongeBob movie!"

"No more SpongeBob movie. You've seen it five times this week and it's only Tuesday."

You know your kids have spent too much time with the Third

Parent when the majority of your toddler's vocabulary has to do with a group of cartoon characters that live in a pineapple under the sea.

It's true! My two-year old can say all the lines WITH the characters. And now he's saying them when the television isn't even on. We're sitting at the table eating lunch and he looks at the empty chair beside him and starts talking to...no one!

"Hi, Bubble Buddy! Hi, SpongeBob!"

"Aiden, eat your sandwich."

"SpongeBob wants a cookie."

"SpongeBob needs to eat his sandwich first." Now I'm talking to imaginary characters....

Like that's a first.

Maybe my son will end up like me—a writer. I hear that repetition is a good thing for toddlers. It helps improve their language. Way back when I was a child we memorized nursery rhymes. Today's kids memorize television shows. But that can work to your advantage as a parent.

Got a cranky toddler in the checkout line? Start singing one of those tunes from Blue's Clues or Dora the Explorer. Toddlers grin like crazy. "Hey, look! Momma swallowed the TV! Do that again, Momma!"

So you go to the dry cleaners, the post office and the bank singing most of the programming for Nickelodeon and the Public Broadcasting System. Before you know it, you have seven more kids toddling along and more moms are encouraging their little ones to join you like you're the in-house nanny.

"How much do you charge?" a mom asks you.

"Oh, I'm not--."

"She's free! It's a free service!" Before you know it, they've roped off that section of the bank, moved in a playhouse, a coloring table and some pop-up books. There just aren't enough graham crackers in your purse to go around.

Somebody tugs on your pant leg. "Hey, Missus, where are the rest of the toys?"

"I wanna color!" "I want a snack!" "I have to go potty!"

Isn't this about the time you wake up in a cold sweat and thank God it was just a dream? Or *was* it?

From the living room you hear the theme song to your toddlers' favorite television show...they're already up and getting their TV fix and you have to drag yourself out of bed and deny them access. So they go ballistic and you start singing the theme song to their favorite show. Then the doorbell rings.

"Is this Mommy's Little Helper Daycare?"

<Close up on mother's face-total shock.>

<Play theme song from The Twilight Zone.>

<Fade to black.>

I'm A Mean Mommy, Yes I Am

If I HAD the money to drop into a 'swear jar' my family would be well on their way to Orlando, Florida by now.

This is the *seventh* time I have had to put back together the closet in my little twerps' (the toddlers) room. For some reason, the entire inventory of *Toys R Us* that they have overflowing from the toy box is not enough to interest them. No, they have moved on to bigger and better things—the only closet in the house where I can store my Stuff.

Yes, that's right, MY Stuff. Stuff that Momma keeps just for herself and doesn't divvy up among all the little chubby outstretched hands. Everything but my chocolate is in there. I hide that under the broccoli. I KNOW that none of the children will look for it there.

But the bulk of my Stuff has to go somewhere and unfortunately it's in munchkin territory.

Things like all my craft supplies, hand-me-down clothes, wrapping paper, china, holiday decorations—you name it, I have it in that closet including a bajillion multi-colored feathers and coins from last year's Mardi Gras party. Can you picture the guilty culprits peering solemnly from beneath a mountain of feathers?

I can just hear brand new parents, fresh from the delivery room, citing some Doctor Whose-It about the fact that my children need more of my attention and this is how they ask for it. Well, I'll tell you what attention they got. Ever see two pint-sized humans sitting in the corner looking miserable? Yes, it's enough to melt even the angriest mom's heart, but I'm not finished with them yet.

I want pain. I want retribution. I want chocolate!!

I hear that stress is a weight accelerant. Great. I have five kids. By the time the youngest graduates from high school I should weigh well over five hundred pounds.

Okay, time to use my brain. Time to put all their toys in the closet and all my Stuff in their toy box. It's a simple matter of reverse psychology. Don't tell me I'm losing my marbles. I never had them anyway. The first boy filched them and has been giving them back to me as birthday gifts ever since.

"Where did you get these?"

"I just found them!"

"WHERE did you find them?"

"On the very top shelf in the back of your closet in a tiny box buried under all those feathers and coins."

You see what I mean? My kids ARE cortisol and they are sticking to my thighs with every incident!

"AIDEN MICHAEL BARKER TURN AROUND!" My littlest is caught trying to enjoy his time in The Chair. "That'll be one more minute in Time Out, mister."

New moms everywhere suck in their breath and flip through their mothering manuals and recite: "Time outs should only be one minute per every year of age."

My two-year old just turned thirty today, did you know that?

My Little Evil Genius

My two-year old impresses us everyday with his developing personality. It's so awesome to watch a child go from being a drooling, needy infant to this independent little hellion.

Today my eight-year old son was busy playing a video game. The two-year old tried to take the controller from his hands, stood between him and the television and basically made a pest of himself.

Older Boy: Knock it off, Aiden. It's not funny!

Younger Boy: Muahahahahaha!

Literally!

Where does this come from? Then my older son warns him, and Aiden zips in, scratches his big brother on the leg and runs down the hall laughing like a maniacal evil genius.

This is the same child that turned over every nook and cranny in my sister's house when we visited, keeping us both on our toes. When he grabbed the telephone and started dialing, she quickly snatched it away from him. And what was he dialing? 666-....

Apparently he was checking in with Command Central.

Maybe we deserve it. His name means "fiery one." That's okay. His cousin's nickname is "Wheels." That's short for Hell On Wheels.

So is it genetics or some sort of chemical transference from clothing? My son wears Wheels' hand-me-downs.

Cousin Wheels is a bit older and recently got a pet fish. In the hands of my kiddo it would be fish paste. As it is he's got plenty to contend with—we have nine cats. These cats do not get to lie around and nap all day. They get plenty of exercise running from the little terror...and, my, they have the longest tails!

I can't believe this is the same child who, only months before, was terrified of heights. Now he scales the bunk beds in seconds flat. And he's such a card. His favorite movie ends and there's this passionate display of heartache—it can't be over!

This is the fifth child and my husband and I take it in stride, but the theatrics are still amazing. This kid has no clue that his older brother and sisters have already tried all the same antics. And now these same antics only make us laugh.

"SpongeBob movie NOW! Juice NOW!"

"But, Aiden, it's time for lunch."

"NO! No, no, no, no, no!"

And we sing: "Do a little dance, make a little noise, get down tonight." Then he's picked up and deposited in his room.

You'd think a tantrum would ensue. But within minutes out comes the charmer and, in a voice so sweet, asks, "Momma, juice? Juice please?"

"No, it's time for nap."

"Nooooo!" (Do a little dance....)

I think having one this age when you are in your thirties is a lot more fun than when you are in your twenties, especially if this isn't your first two-year old. How else can you be entertained by such raw talent? We ought to make some videos. We've got a lot of material for blackmail in the future.

Unexpected Silly Moments

I'm sick of the 'diaper whoofs.' You know what they are. Diaper whoofs are the false alarm when you think your baby has filled his diaper. First you cup his bottom and then you peek down the back of his diaper...only to be knocked dead by a ghost poopy. You look, but even though the smoke detector is screaming because of the smell, there's nothing to change.

My youngest is now old enough to know when his bottom has burped and he always shoots me a grin after I've been knocked over by one. Is it genetically a boy thing? Are males created with desire to have their finger pulled?

The next stage of 'entertainment' is when the children start blowing raspberries on their arms. What's funnier—the sound or fooling Momma?

40

"All right. That's enough."

"PBFFFFFFFFFFFFFFFT!" (Chortles and shrills of laughter.)

What's a parent to do but join in the fun?

"Pbbbbbbbt-bbbbt-bbt!" I shoot back.

There is something about a parent acting silly that brings out the best in kids. And it makes perfect sense. Being silly is a great stress buster. And more adults would benefit from acting like kids more often, I think. In fact, I've drawn up a treatise of exercises adults must perform weekly for sound health.

#1 Blow bubbles in your chocolate milk.

#2 Jump up and down on the bed.

#3 Stomp in mud puddles.

#4 Blow raspberries on your arm.

#5 Have a Godzilla-burp contest.

#6 Have an ice cream sundae for breakfast once a month.

#7 Sing out loud, sing out strong!

#8 Go barefoot.

#9 Run through the sprinklers with all your clothes on.

#10 Snap your gum as loud as you can.

Ever notice how we're told NOT to do these things when we are kids...and then when we grow up we're so stressed out that we go to therapy and we're told to do these very same things to recapture childlike wonder, spontaneity and a sense of humor?

Sometimes it takes something otherwise mundane or dreaded to spark a little silliness in our lives. I say, go for it! Let your kids inspire you. Do they *really* need to stop whatever it is they are doing?

Why don't you fall over and roll on the floor and "die dramatically" the next time the baby needs his pants changed? Odds are the other little ones will copy you and a sour diaper could turn into a few moments of giggling with all the children.

That's all it takes. Just a little thinking and acting outside the box.

I have to go now...there's a pack of gum and a sprinkler out there with my name on it.

Chapter Two

~Older Kids~

My Sanity Is Being Held Hostage

Talent Overflowing At This House

I was visiting my favorite online message board where I hang out with a bunch of other moms, and I was sharing the latest about my kids.

Then it hit me! Am I running a three-ring circus or what?

Yep, there's the bearded lady, there's the two-headed chicken and there is my two-year old jamming his finger in the top of his eye so that he nearly pops it out.

How can he DO that!?!?!

And along comes one of my eleven-year old daughters announcing that today she only fell on her face ONCE. This is a great feat considering that only days ago she ran into a parked car and gouged a good chunk of skin off her knee.

But let's not forget my three-year old. Now *here* is raw talent. She can suck her thumb and pick both nostrils at the same time...with ONE hand!

Let's have a round of applause!

Should I be worried? Should I be more concerned?

Heck, no. All this is pretty sane compared to the antics of my bipolar eight-year old son. But today he's having a relatively *normal* day. Today he is just another male lost in the confusing labyrinth that is called WOMAN, heedless of the Minotaur that waits for him, preying on him. (Did you know that the Minotaur was actually FEMALE?)

He so desperately wants to be friends with the pack of kindergarten girls on our street that he keeps going back for more pain and punishment. They tease, they confuse him with their mercurial moods, and they steal his toys and break his heart over and over and over again. Never mind that *I've* warned him time and time again, men on the street just shake their heads when he gets his feelings hurt and I even hear them pass on this timeless wisdom: "They're *GIRLS*."

Like that's supposed to mean something.

What *does* it mean?

I know it means *something*. I instinctively know that it's a reference to the confusion women have left men in since the dawn of time.

But does my son get it?

Noooooooooo. Back he goes for more. And the grown men wipe their greased stained hands on their oily rags and peep from under the hoods of their cars as my son valiantly marches up to the girls and makes a plea for their attention.

They erupt into a cascade of giggles and he stands there perplexed. Evel Knievel had nothing on my kid. He jumped ten cars? Twenty? My son would leap from the earth to the moon just to know the joy of friendship with these little women.

Ah, but there is a lesson about the difference in the sexes that he must experience for decades before he can truly appreciate and respect it...and then tune out while he watches the game on television.

For now he is happy with the ten minutes of attention they fawn on him.

Meanwhile, I need to check on my other eleven-year old, the acrobat who glides through the trees with greatest of ease until she lands on her back impaled on a limb. That was a memorable summer.

And just where is that two-year old?

Something rolls across the floor.

Oh, *GREAT*, is that an eye or a marble!?!?

Where's The Briefs?

My eldest son is eight-years old. Now I know that kids at that age through twelve, especially boys, will stop washing so they can cultivate a nice layer of grease and filth over their bodies.

And I know that most walk around with their flies open. It's just that there's so much to learn, so much to absorb at that age, who can be bothered with such small details like zipping up one's fly?

And these days, it goes well with the intended fashion statement of wearing one's pants two inches lower than one's briefs.

But I'm not complaining that my son has taken up this lose-the-belt-look. Oh, no. I think I could understand that one. Even though I detest the excuse that "Everybody else is doing it." At least I could understand *that* reasoning in some way.

No, my son has come up with another fashion faux pas. He

doesn't wear any underwear.

Hey, it's just too much trouble to put them on!

Which gets me to thinking…why *do* we wear underwear anyway?

To protect the outer clothes? I'll buy that. After seeing what an eight-year old boy can do to the inside of a pair of jeans when he doesn't wear his underwear…which has something to do with not bothering to waste time with bathroom tissue….

What gives?

"Son, why aren't you wearing underwear?"

"I don't know."

"What do you mean you don't know? Didn't you realize you didn't have any underwear with you when you were dressing in the bathroom this morning?"

"Uh-huh."

"Then, why didn't you go back to your room and get a pair of underwear?"

"I don't know."

"Do you *like* not wearing underwear?"

"No."

"Didn't you notice that you haven't been wearing them all day?"

"Uh-huh."

"Then WHY didn't you go get some and put them on?"

"I don't know!"

Why I try to get to the bottom of these things I don't know. Maybe it's because I'm a mom and it's my job to make sure my kids are wearing clean underwear at all times, as if should anyone else ever find out the contrary, it will be decided that I am somehow an unfit mother because my children aren't *wearing* any underwear.

And I can just see my mother, her mother and her mother's mother shaking their heads in shame. "What kind of mother *is* she? The boy didn't even have on any underwear."

It's part of the genetic make-up of mothers. Not only are we authorities on pig sties, it is our God-given duty to make sure all our children wear underwear and they had better be clean.

Section IV, Article VII of the Mother's Handbook clearly states that ALL CHILDREN SHALL WEAR UNDERWEAR AT ALL TIMES AND IT HAD BETTER BE CLEAN.

But try getting that through to my son.

He just gives me a faraway look, like his mind is already out riding his bike and soon this harbinger-creature that gave birth to him, that is now squawking over him and giving him the third degree, will release him so he can go outside to play.

Who needs underwear anyway?

Time to talk about IBS

Let's be frank and discuss something that all too many people find uncomfortable—IBS, or, as we moms call it: "Irritable Boy Syndrome."

For far too long it has been the girls that shoulder the weight of unpredictable hormones and mood swings even though many of us have grown up with brothers that were equally as temperamental.

In my case, I now have *two* sons that qualify as being stricken with IBS. The eight-year old will burst into tears or fits of anger at the drop of a hat. The two-year old is a never-ending wailing English ambulance siren. What's a mother to do?

I can't talk it out with my eldest son. He will burst into tears and cry, "I caaaaan't!" And the youngest just wants to cling to me like a monkey, afraid that if he lets go, I will disappear into the bathroom never to return. (And some days he has good reason to fear this, let me tell you!)

There is certainly no doubt that once they discover this column and realize it's about them, there's going to be a cold front that will last for months. Hmmmm. Maybe I just solved my problem. The silent treatment I can live with at this point.

Nobody ever told me raising boys would be like this! In fact, my grandmother insists that boys are easier to raise than girls. I'd like to know how!

Perhaps it's true and the boys will eventually outgrow this stage. Unlike girls, who have to succumb to the 'crankies' because they are at the mercy of a cycle for this and a cycle for that for the rest of their lives.

Have you ever had a man ask you if the clothes he is wearing make him look fat? Have you men ever had your buddy burst into tears because his wife didn't pack him the right kind of sandwich? At some point the male will outgrow the waterworks. I believe that.

What I want to know is WHEN this is going to happen?! I can't take anymore! It's getting so bad that when my husband comes home from work and asks me how my day went all I can say is" I-I-I-I don-n-n-n-n-n't kno-o-o-o-o--w!" Everything is a whine from me. I have to purge. It's all I hear anymore!

I'm lying in bed at night and I hear it in my sleep. "Mo-m-m-m-m-m-m! I ne-e-e-e-e-e-d you-u-u-u-u-u!" And my husband can't sleep because I'm yelling at the kids in my dreams.

Try sleeping with a woman that keeps bursting out with: "Knock it off already!"

"But I haven't tried anything yet, dear!"

The worst part about the whinies is that no matter who has them, they are contagious. I might have a happy houseful, but then a few more come home from school, and one starts in with the whinies, and the next thing I know all five are whining!

Now, I've seen this ad on television that claims it can cure IBS. I thought I'd give them a call. How much should I give to an eight-year old boy and his two-year old accomplice? Will it induce sleep? And if it does, *HOW SOON?*

After twenty minutes of my questions, their customer service person responded: "I don-n-n-n-n-n't kno-w-w-w-w-w!"

I'll just have to suck it up and deal with it until these boys are grown.

My Kids are Liars? No!

I walked into the kitchen the other day and found one of our kittens standing on her hind legs on top of a footstool trying to reach for things on the counter.

While I stood, amazed, she quickly showed me a few other things she'd learned, like how to sample cupcakes and eat leftovers from lunch all while leaving evidence that suspiciously looked as if one of the children had been up to no good.

Ever notice that how kids and pets play off one another? They can either be partners in crime or public enemy number one to each other. It all depends on what favor the odds are. When it comes to stealing food, all is fair game.

Mom: "Who was into the cupcakes?"

Children: " Do you think it was one of the cats?"

See? It's the power of suggestion. I can't blame a child if there is any reasonable doubt and the kids *know* this. It's one of my weaknesses. My husband doesn't have that problem because he doesn't care. That's his job, to not care, because he is the father. I'm the mother, the emotional one. I care about everything far too much and far too long afterward when everyone else has forgotten it.

My husband's motto is: "All children are guilty until proven innocent." This works for him. Like I said, he's the FATHER. The kids expect this and even look at me like I'm nuts if I try to plea-bargain for them. So I've learned my place. It's somewhere between "Hey, what's going on here?" and "If I find out it's you, there's going to be trouble!"

My husband is the heavy. He thinks the incontrovertible evidence that the children are guilty is BECAUSE the children are guilty.

I'm the soft mush. No one listens to me! Threats from mom are just the fluff that comes with the territory. All my evidence is circumstantial.

Child: "Mom, are you absolutely sure that it was me or could one of the cats have knocked over that vase?"

That I even give it a moment's consideration means I've lost the case. So I've got to be even sneakier than the kids to win my day in court.

Mom: "Somebody has been in the cookie jar."

Child: "Um, I saw one of the cats over there a while ago."

Mom: "I can't believe those cats would do such a thing!"

Child: "Remember, um, the, ah, cupcakes?"

Mom: "I guess the cats really like oatmeal raisin..."

Child: "I thought they were chocolate—"

Mom: "Ah-HA!"

I might be the light-weight feather-brain around here when it comes to pleading cases, but I've got MOM RADAR that can trap a kid in a lie faster than super glue can stick your hands together. (Don't ask.) All I've got to do now is bring the evidence to my husband and the kids are sunk. The consequences will be meted out. The case is closed.

Yep, it's a trait that moms have possessed since the dawn of time. For ages kids have been tripping over 'ums' and 'ahs' whenever mom's radar locks in on them. And they'll be doing it for a long time to come.

And yet, time and time again, it amazes me that these sweet children I carried for nine-months would LIE to me! It's enough to bring a mom to tears, which brings up a mom's other secret weapon: GUILT. But that's another story.

Mysteries of the Laundry Pile

Why is it that my kids need me to wash their favorite sweatshirt or jeans five days a week, but if I left it up to them they wouldn't change their bed sheets more than once a year?

Why do socks go in as pairs and come out as singles?

Why can't M&M's make their candy able to withstand the heat of the dryer? Melts in your mouth and not in the permanent press cycle.

Why is it that only one leg of a pair of stockings gets wrapped around the agitator in the washer making half of the pair long enough for a ten-foot-tall woman?

How do my husband's black socks keep slipping into the load of whites to be bleached? He has a nice set of purple undergarments going there.

How come I can't pull the loose threads on my dishtowels, but the minute I put them in the washer they pull and get tangled with everything else…like that ten-foot leg of pantyhose?

How do Weebles end up at the bottom of every load?

Just how many outfits does Barbie go through in a day? And does she have to wear Velcro? I'm tired of her clothes sticking to my ten-foot stockings.

Why do sweat socks smell like corn chips? How can my children wear their socks just once and yet those socks can totally stand up on their own when taken off?

Why can the very article of clothing somebody's looking for end up at the bottom of the damp laundry basket smelling like tuna? And why is it the very article of clothing that MUST be worn in five minutes?

Why do my kids spend thirty minutes slicking their hair straight and walk out the door to school with shirts that look slept in?

How do red shirts end up in the whites EVERY TIME?

Why don't I believe that the portion size of soap the box suggests is going to be strong enough for the load I'm washing? Don't these laundry soap manufacturers have kids?

Why is it that a load of laundry takes thirty minutes to dry until it has my baby's 'blankie' in it and then it takes forever? And how do you explain to a hysterical child that 'blankie' is coming back?

Whose idea was it to put pockets on the jeans of little boys and tomboys anyway?

Why does the cat keep trying to get in the washer? Should I let her go for a spin?

How can I harness the joy my two-year old has when he runs to open the dryer, empty it and stick his head inside to yell and hear the echo?

How do I convince my kids that my lopsided ten-foot stockings are not for tug-o-war?

And, finally, who keeps filling up those hampers the very minute I have everything washed, dried, folded and put away?

Summer Vacation Fun

The kids all want to go to Disneyland, but I don't see what the big deal is. I mean, it's not like we don't ever go anywhere fun. Don't they remember Laundryland?

"Mom, this is BORING."

"Hey, now I just paid EIGHT quarters for you to view the wash through a front loading machine window. And look…you're the right height for the dryers. Hurry up or you'll miss the permanent press cycle!"

"But we want to see Mickey Mouse."

"Keep your eyes open. Laundryland has plenty of mice."

"Can we have lunch?"

"What—you don't like the snack machine?"

Kids. They're so ungrateful. You take them to the movies and they have to blab their age to everyone…right when I'm explaining that my very tall "five-year old" has a gland condition. And, yes. I'm usually thirty pounds heavier when we go due to the snacks strapped to my middle under a really big sweatshirt. "Hey, make sure you cough when you pop that soda tab," I warn them.

You fill up a garbage can for the kids to swim in during the summer and they scream because there are a few bugs in the water. You take them to the mall and buy them a pretzel…and they complain because you didn't divide it evenly five ways. They say they want to go to a water park, so you hose down the slide and tell them to go for it.

Kids just don't appreciate much these days.

When I was a kid I'd wade barefoot in the sewer for fun. I'd spend hours in my playhouse—an old refrigerator box. And every weekend my parents would take me to the park…and to pass the time they'd bet on the horses.

It can be tricky planning the perfect summer activities that please the whole family, but it can be done. Just keep these tips in mind:

1. Glad bags work as a slip-and-slide if you stretch them out and water them down properly, but don't anchor them with rocks at the end of the 'slide.' Your kids can lose a few teeth that way.

2. If you let the kids have water balloons hold a few back for yourself and wait until they use all theirs…then let them have it.

3. When camping...stake your tent as close to the back door as possible so you can slip into the house and sleep in your own bed once the kids fall asleep.

4. When the kids have a sleepover don't let them watch the scariest movie ever or the chances are good that hyped-up pre-teen girls will beat you to a pulp on your way to the bathroom.

5. Always stand five feet away from the barbecue pit when the kids are toasting marshmallows unless you're good at penciling in your eyebrows.

When it comes to summer vacation fun, keep a list of chores on hand. I guarantee the kids will appreciate what you have planned that much more.

Phone High Jinks – Or What Goes Around Comes Around

The minute you pick up the phone the kids are there. "Mom, I need to know the meaning of life and I need to know NOW!!"

If they aren't begging for your undivided attention, then they are marching around like a Sousa band in the background. The net result is a phone conversation peppered with covert parental threats to "Keep it down or else!" or the injection of inappropriate bodily sounds from the children every time you pause to try to think straight.

"Hi, Mary?" The band strikes up, the wind section heralding the commencement of the parade, and here comes the baton twirler....

"I wanted to know if you knew … Put that down! … how many cookies were needed for the … Put it down NOW … bake sale?"

Baton twirler scoots just out of reach as cymbals crash and drum major approaches with question that must be answered now!

"Six dozen? ... Not now...just a minute! ... No, hi, sorry, Mary...the kids..."

"PLEEEEEASE, PLEASE, PLEASE, PLEASE, MOMMY?"

"*Yes*, I said, yes, already...No, Mary, I'm sorry, not you, um, I mean, yes, I can bake six dozen..." CRASH! The band is building up for the big finale. Whatever you just agreed to with one of the kids happens to result in spilled milk accompanied by a lot of crying.

"Mom, the dog is eating the cookies you just baked..!"

"Um, no, Mary, it won't be any (BELCH!) trouble ... What's the matter with you? (LAUGHTER) at all."

"Mom, Johnny just snorted milk out his nose—look he's doing it again!"

"Uh, Mary, (SNORRRRRT!) I'll have to get (PBBBBBBBBBFT!) back to you...."

So that's a pretty typical phone call in my house. That's why it was hysterical the day my eldest daughter was on the phone excusing herself from a 4-H meeting. It happened to be right in the middle of what I call 'rush hour.' 5PM to 7PM in my house is noisy and carefully orchestrated chaos. In laymen's terms, it's dinnertime.

So my poor daughter attempts to make this phone call right at ground zero—the kitchen—where mom is cooking, toddlers are whining, siblings are all placing last minute bids on mom's shot nerves, the cats are blocking off the exits lest I escape without tripping over them and breaking my neck and the dog is dancing in place because he needs to go outside.

My daughter very carefully and succinctly says: "My sister and I can't attend the meeting tonight because—"

"THERE'S POOP ON THE FLOOR! YOU BETTER NOT GET POOP ALL OVER THE PLACE!"

That was me. She was sooooooo red with embarrassment. I'm not sure she even finished leaving the message. She just sort of shrank away and died, mortified.

Me? I couldn't stop laughing. It takes awhile, but eventually we moms get even—and without any planning. Someday my daughter will be able to look back on this and laugh. Until then, "I'm laughing WITH you honey, not at you!"

Three Sounds That Make Mom Run

There are only three sounds that send a full-grown mother running. They are:

*Screams of terror and pain

*Silence

*Yakking

Screams of terror and pain. These screams stand out among all the other screams and cries children make. A scream of terror or pain is a very primal scream that, no matter what a mom is doing, it seizes her hips, rotates her toward the source and compels her legs to start running.

There's a BIG difference in a scream like this that sets it apart from all others. In fact a mom can probably tell you upon hearing the very first note just what the injury or fright entails. It doesn't matter how old the child is, this is a job for Mom alone.

Silence. Any good mom worth her salt will tell you that the sound of silence is a sound worthy of panic. Whether she has one child or a dozen, the minute the house, or the yard or the street suddenly goes quiet, Mom knows that *somebody* is up to no good and she is summoned by the silence and *must* discover the reason for it.

The sound of silence is very much like the sound of guilt, something that mothers are very adept at interpreting since they live with their own abundant supply and have plenty to dish out. If only children realized that silence gives away their misdeeds, they could get away with so much more.

In fact, if they'd just bicker and babble while they were up to no good, a parent would never be any the wiser. But children are not yet able to master doing two things at one time, and that is completely in a mom's favor.

Yakking. Whether it's a child or a pet, a mom can hear the sound of upchucking from a dead sleep or in the middle of any racket. The urge is always to grab a towel and run while she yells for everyone to clear the room so she can isolate the yakker and the messy results.

You don't want pets or little ones poking around inquisitively when there is an active yakker in the house.

And yet, there's always an audience with at least one informant that stands and gawks and states the obvious through the whole ordeal:

"Mom, the cat is yakking!"

"Mom, the cat yakked!"

"Eew! Mom, the baby is touching it!"

"Mom, you're cleaning that yak, huh?"

"Wow, what a mess…."

Needless to say, all this is why no matter how much a mother complains from time to time, the truth is that the sound of babbling, squawking and bickering is music to her ears. It means that all is well!

Chapter Three

~Out In Public~

What Was I Thinking?!

Divide And Conquer

I should know better. When darting out the door for a quick run to the store, be ruthless in denying kids who chime in that they want to go with you.

Never take more than two--and that's asking for it.

Ever notice that? You go to the store with one kid and you get the low down of every kid in the school and all the goings-on in the neighborhood. Take two and you get bickering. Take three or four and you end up with ballerinas in the aisles, sticky fingers in the candy and magazine centers and too many hands helping the bagger at the check out.

Yes, I know. Five kids is A LOT OF KIDS to some people!

Not me. I love it all.

That, however, does not mean I am without strategy. All the kids get a reminder before we go into the store. It's true. You walk in with one kid in a pair of jeans and a t-shirt and it's nothing new under the sun. He might pick his nose, he might even whine a bit, but no one really notices.

You walk in with five kids and suddenly 'that mom doesn't have enough sense to clean her kids up, buy them some new clothes, teach them some manners, yadda yadda yadda'. Don't even get me started on people full of free advice about birth control. (My husband and I like to black out our teeth before we go out with all the kids in tow.)

So here I was with my five. They got The Reminder in the car before we left. "We're a big family. People notice. Be on your best behavior. Show them the good points about big families. Okay, ready? Let's go!"

Child #4 contorts herself backward when placed in the shopping cart. Noooooooooooo! She wants to walk with the big kids...which means, running helter-skelter through the aisles like she's possessed.

Child #3 pirouettes and hops in and out and around the basket...and on my FEET!

Child #2 gets lost.

Child #1, who should know better, starts examining each item on display at the check out.

Mom says syrupy-sweetly to her, "And where do we place our hands when we are at the store? On our tummies! *Yes*, good job!"

Okay, ONE kid gets the message--sarcasm is not lost! But I am afraid it was all in vain...as I hear myself go on--and I SWEAR I see

adults around us mouthing my words--have they heard it all before???
Have we been to the store too many times that day, er, week already?

"Look all you want with your eyes, but not your hands."

"Stop hopping on that man's foot."

"No, you cannot eat that right here, Momma has to pay for it first."

"No, we are not buying/getting/going to/coming back for that today."

"No, no, no," coupled with, "Stop teasing, don't touch, what did I tell you, if I told you once-I've told you 100 times…"

Get the picture?

More importantly, do I?

Sure! Divide and conquer. Never take more than will be helpful. Have I learned my lesson?

Probably not.

How To Make Your Toddler Possessed

I rarely take my kids on a clothes-shopping expedition--unless it's for the child in tow and all the rest are at home. This means I have a 90% record in my favor of happy, well-behaved kids when shopping for clothes.

Unlike me when I was a child, my kids aren't running through the aisles, or ensconcing themselves in the middle of a circular rack...and consequently aren't getting their hair lengthened when mom seizes their ponytails and pulls. HARD.

I have kids who actually look forward to clothes shopping.

That is, until today.

I haven't been shopping seriously for clothes for myself since my twins (now eleven) were about the age of their youngest sister now who's three. That was back in the days when just about the time I was completely down to my undergarments one or both of the twins would whip open the curtain of the changing room, much to my chagrin and the surprise of all the other customers in the vicinity. Whee!

So, eight years later, I'm a little wiser and REALLY desperate. Down to the two little ones, I tuck them in the double stroller and embark on my daring mission to seek clothes for my new body. After five kids, it's a new body.

Well, we're at my favorite store--the one where I mooned everyone eight years ago. I'm relatively sure that no one remembers me. I riffle through the racks like a clerk at the post office sorting mail. Yep, nope, maybe, nope, nope, YES!

Once I accumulate a load of 'yesses', I pile them on the stroller and park the kids just out of arm's reach of the dressing curtain. I'm fast, I'm greased lightening and I'm in and out of outfits so fast I'm busting a sweat. And then it starts.

At first it sounded like the low growl of a finely tuned Caddy. But it begins to build and crescendo with vehemence. I peek out of the curtain just in time to see the sweet blonde head of my three-year old rotate 360 degrees. Her eyes cross, that deep guttural growl sounds again and then--Yipes! I duck back before the pea soup can hit my new skirt.

I know, I know. Seven hours shopping for clothes, no matter how many cookie bribes I made, no matter that we took a lunch break and no matter that Momma got them each a plush dog were just a wee bit too much for these kiddos. The three-year old is trying to take her two-year old brother's head off (she sits behind him in the stroller) while he's simultaneously attempting to scalp her.

Okay. Time to go. Wait...just one more thing!

BWAAAAAAAAAAAAAAAAAAAAAAAAAH.

Snorrrrrrrrrrrrrrrrrrrrrrrrrre.

One is possessed. One is out cold.

We check out. It'll be months before these two won't shriek when they see a rack of clothes.

But hey, good news! One skirt was half off...and the toys were free!

I'll Show You

Does anybody else have a kid or two bent on showing you who is the boss?

I've got a very bright eight-year old who 'has a problem with authority'. He only respects the sergeant voice. I do use my sergeant voice...but there are times when I can hear myself begin to whine especially when I have to stand my ground with this child for the UPTEENTH time.

So two weeks ago we are shopping for clothes for the kids. It's our yearly duty. I have to postpone it to an annual event because there just isn't money all those other times--when the sales are even better.

Well, lo and behold, the first and closest department is the girls' department. My girls are just about finished getting all the 'must haves' on their lists. It will only take twenty minutes for them to make their selections.

But twenty minutes is twenty minutes too long for a bipolar child who 'has a problem with authority.' And I'm in a 'get in and get it done' mood so I am in no frame of mind to A) cater to his whims (and that rarely happens anyway) or B) pound him with my drill sergeant's voice. So naturally, he ups the ante. If Mom isn't going to DROP EVERYTHING NOW and take me to the boys' department to get MY PANTS, then I am going to PUNISH her by getting myself 'lost'.

Oh, yes. It's the old 'hide in the aisles and run from your mother with a deaf and blind look on your face until you really *are* lost' strategy.

Fifteen minutes later the woman at the desk where the changing rooms are tells me my little boy is up front. I say, "Good, he can wait there."

She says into the phone, "Mom says he can wait there."

I can just hear my son suck in his breath from across the store acreage. How dare she!

I say, "He is just punishing me. He's being a brat. I will come get him when I am finished."

And the woman actually repeats into the phone what I say verbatim. I know my son is hearing this and reconsidering his plan to assume command of our outing.

Well, what's a mom to do? When you have two toddlers in two different carts and two eleven-year old kiddos changing in two different dressing rooms and ONE child trying to drum up the pity for himself up front, do you cave or stand your ground?

I could have HUGGED the woman for telling the people up front that he was just being a brat. I'm sure my son heard. It still makes me laugh.

So we left the store that day without any clothing for my son, who spent his clothes changing time up front sitting with the store clerks.

Maybe by August he'll have the patience it takes to wait five minutes to get his clothes, try them on and pay for it. Or maybe he won't. But sooner or later he'll need pants because the shorts just won't keep him warm. He'll come around.

I'll show *him*.

A Run-in With The Parent Police

So there I was…in the middle of the bra aisle with the three-year old and two-year old in tow. I'd played it smart. I had both children strapped into a shopping cart of their own. I had them parked out of range of the merchandise.

I knew my size. I deftly hunted for the appropriate color, whisked it into a cart and weaved my way from women's lingerie to skivvies for the kiddies.

It was looking as if my Underwear Mission would soon be Mission Accomplished…but nooooooooooooooooooo.

Somewhere between the trainer slingshots for my eleven-year old daughters and the black dress socks for my eldest boy, I noticed this strange trail of plastic cards. Hmmmmm, that looks just like…MY ATM CARD! MY CREDIT CARD! MY DRIVER'S LICENSE!

ACK!!!

Grinning like a happy hamster, my two-year old demonstrated how the contents of my wallet had been strewn along like a plan Hansel and Gretel had hatched to help Mommy find her way back to the Bra Department…by smoothly tossing the little important slips of paper and money in my purse up in the air like confetti!

Of COURSE, I knew my priorities.

I immediately abandoned my kids as I desperately tried to collect all my most important personal and financial tokens. You'd think I was a mad woman on a treasure hunt in the aisles of unmentionables.

Satisfied that I had retrieved all my things before my identity could be stolen, I returned to my children only to discover a 'helpful' fellow shopper standing there to inform me that my two-year old had stood up in his seat.

"Really? There's a first. He's never stood before. In fact, we thought we'd have to carry him all his life."

LIKE I CARE! What's a broken neck compared to stolen identity, maxed out credit cards and a bank account swiftly drained? I can have more children, but can I ever salvage my credit history?

It's not that I didn't care. I do. I just love it when a stranger decides to be helpful by being critical. I should never leave my kids alone. I should make sure they sit at all times. I KNOW THAT!

SHE had no idea what I had been up to. It was as if she thought I'd just decided to park my kids in the middle of nowhere and stroll off to browse and have a jolly good time. Like, "Eh, somebody will come along and baby sit for me…."

Well, thanks to her valuable insight, I am now an INFORMED (or is it REFORMED?) mother and my kids will never be neglected or abandoned again when I shop. The world can once again rotate on its axis.

Yeah, right. Where will this woman be when I am trying to change one toddler while the other runs out of the restroom and willy-nilly through the rest of the mall? Oh, I know! She'll be holding the hand of my runaway with this dour expression as if to say, "Woman, don't you know that a child can be kidnapped in mere seconds? Why are you just allowing her to run around unsupervised?"

"DUHHHHHHHHHHH, I don't know!"

Does any member of the Parenting Police People ever stop and look at the whole situation? And where are THEIR children anyway? Do they even HAVE children?

You never see a critic with a child in tow. In fact, you never GET criticism from another parent with child in tow. Instead, you get this look, that knowing wink, that nod of solidarity. A parent never assumes that the other parent is incompetent. In fact, some look for ways to help or commiserate.

But Parenting Police People are convinced that you should have never had children to begin with. They will shake their heads and cluck their tongues, offer you unsolicited advice about birth control or state the obvious.

"Your child is running through the aisles."

82

"You mean this isn't Disneyland?"

"Your child is standing in his seat."

"Amazing! He's working without a net!"

"Is it naptime?"

"No, they always scream like this."

"You must have your hands full."

"No, I just like to drop bottles of milk on the floor to see how fast it takes the clerk to call out WET SPILL ON AISLE THREE!"

"Your son has a potty mouth."

"My husband and I think self-expression is $%#&*@ GOOD for them."

"These children are all yours?"

"So THAT explains why they keep following me home!"

Well, we made it to the check-out without anybody calling Child Protective Services. At least for now, sarcasm isn't viewed as parental incompetence.

Stupidity, The Bane of All Parents

When it comes to parenting pet peeves, one thing most parents can't stand is stupidity in children.

I'm not talking about the usual brainless things that happen around the house that you EXPECT with children, things like spilled milk, kids lolling all over the sofa instead of sitting like regular human beings, clothes that never make it two feet to the hamper, and a myriad of half-baked chores that never quite get done; things you have to stand over children and cite the obvious, repeatedly, all so they can ignore you and continue on in blissful ignorance.

I'm talking about DUMB things like walking through the house with a plastic bat whacking yourself in the head over and over and over.

That's my two-year old. (Bonk!) "Ow." (Bonk!) "Ow." (Bonk!) "Ow." I have to take the bat away before he gives himself a

84

concussion.

What about hurrying up to get ahead of your mom or dad in the hallway just so you can slow down to a crawl and get tripped over?

Or following so closely BEHIND Mom that when she stops, you find yourself back in the womb?

How about walking into walls? Why do kids do that? "Bibble bibble bobble boo," they babble and 'bonk!' into the wall they go. And they don't even cry. It's just 'bonk!' and repeat and then change course like one of those battery operated cars they make for kids these days...and all the while they keep on babbling.

Ever notice that? When you EXPECT your kids to get hurt, they don't. You watch your kids play at the park. They fall off slides, out of trees, off the jungle gym. They run into walls and signs posts. They get up and start running and do it all over again. Then they walk two feet and trip and here come the waterworks. What does this tell us? That science is wrong about physics? No, it tells us that kids are, well, sometimes complete idiots.

And the reason that parents hate this is because odds are somebody is going to think our children take right after us. Am I right?

Like somebody is out there thinking, "Man, I bet that mom just loves going around the house whacking herself in the head with a blunt object."

Well, actually I do. I'm having one of those days today. All anybody seems to be able to do is whine. There are NO WORDS! It's just whiiii-iii-iiii-ne about this and that and everything in between.

WHY????? I don't know! (Bonk, bonk, bonk!)

Here's one. If you put your finger in the cat's mouth, it will get bitten. That's a no-brainer! And yet the same child will put the same finger in the cat's mouth three times more immediately after getting bitten...and cry about it!

"Momma, it hurts when I do this!"

"Then, don't DO that!"

What about walking on sidewalks? My kids (all five of them) can't walk on a sidewalk to save their lives without tripping into somebody's garden or falling into the street. And THREE of my children are older than seven years!

I'm SURE that the neighbors are thinking, "Man, idiocy just RUNS in that family! What kind of person can't walk down a sidewalk?" And here we are, a whole family, putting on a prime show for those behind-the-curtain-peeping neighbors.

So I'm sitting with my foot on ice today because I fell off the sidewalk on the way to the mailbox this morning... and I'm thinking about a parent's fear of stupidity and getting labeled as such.

Bumps and bruises are like nicks and scrapes on any inanimate object. If you treat your property that way, it shows you don't care. And when it comes to kids, if they end up with all these bumps and bruises, we must be doing something wrong!

But we aren't. And we can't stop them.

The best we can do is buy some kneepads and helmets hoping we'll help our kids escape the Darwin effect...so they don't kill themselves walking down the hall.

And when they reach the age of twenty-five we can congratulate ourselves because our kids SURVIVED childhood.

Now pass me a cookie because my foot is *really* throbbing!

These Boots Were Made For Shopping

Give me an hour, twenty bucks, and a shopping cart at the Dollar Store and you'll have one happy Momma.

Where else can a mom of five go shopping and feel like she's made of millions? Hey, I can afford EVERYTHING at the dollar store! And when I'm feeling particularly generous, I'll even buy EACH OF THE KIDS a treat. Whoa, look out! It's Mommy Warbucks!

So I was at the Dollar Store the other day scoping out the items I'd be back for sans kiddos. I was planning my "Santa Stocking Stuffer" shopping expedition...something I'd have to do later with my two toddlers who have no long-term memory.

They're great! I can take them through toy store after toy store, get their opinion on every single item, pile toys and books in the cart, bring them home and wrap the presents in front of them and just a few weeks later…GENUINE SURPRISE!

But short-term memory, on the other hand, has its drawbacks. Especially when it's mine and I'm severely lacking in it. (When am I going to learn?)

I take my toddlers to the Dollar Store and THIS time I don't put each in a separate cart. I try to save time by putting the two-year old in the seat and the three-year old in the cart itself—with the items I'm buying.

I'm stocking up on necessities for around the house, boring things like dish soap and barbecue sauce. While I'm debating which salad dressings I'll buy, I hear "blub, blub, blub" and I'm not smart enough to figure it out instantaneously, I actually think, "Hey, that's sort of a catchy…TUNE!" It's my three-year old with the dish soap, cap off, bottle completely upside down, standing in the cart with a big grin on her face pouring soap all over the other items.

I start mumbling furiously under my breath, something which tends to make me look like a chicken, especially when I get my head going side-to-side and my hair, twisted up loosely in the back, starts bobbing. My daughter breaks up in little cackles…I'm slipping all over the floor while I try to push the cart out of the orange soap puddle and the little one, pleased with Mommy's performance, cheers and exclaims: "Bubble!"

Yes, there are bubbles everywhere and Don Ho comes to life on the intercom…something about a luau on aisle five, but I'm not sticking around for it. I leave a conspicuous trail of orange dish soap from the aisle to the checkout and the cashier asks if I'd like another bottle.

"No, we'll take this one."

Why do I say that? Especially when it's not going to cost anybody more than a few pennies? Because it's the principle of the thing. My daughter spilled about twenty-seven cents worth. That means I still have seventy-three cents left and I'll be darned if I'm going to waste that.

Hey, I might be Mommy Warbucks at the Dollar Store, but when it comes to pinching pennies, I'm still Scrooge, still watching that budget and still making every cent count.

Besides, I've got to hurry home and bathe my barbecue sauce and salad dressings and use up the soap I rinse off of them to do a whole load of dishes.

Tell Don I'll have to take a rain check.

When Visiting With Little Ones...

We visited my parents again over the Labor Day weekend.

Mom, as usual, had more food than a small army could consume. I was in heaven.

    1) I didn't have to cook.

    2) I didn't have to do dishes.

    3) I didn't have to cook.

And that's how it is for moms. No sooner do you finish cleaning up after one meal than you have to start thinking of the next. If you don't, then you find you have a house full of hungry people staring at you like you're the only edible thing for miles around.

You've got to keep the natives from getting restless.

Well, I know what this perpetual meal planning will do to me. I'm going to turn into my mom. Sometimes she is already PREPARING the following meal while we are still taking up our first plate of the meal at hand.

So we visited my parents over the holiday weekend. The kids traveled well. I guess the little ones are getting used to long distance riding.

However, once we got there, the toddlers were like mice on speed until it was time to duct tape them and tuck them in for the night.

Ever notice that? When you travel, the kids sleep. You can't. You and your spouse stay awake, talking, keeping each other alert, and you even relish the quiet. Hey, the children are ASLEEP and you're AWAKE! How often does THAT happen? I mean, how often does it happen that the kids are sleeping and you are awake with enough energy to do more than grunt and sit on the sofa with the remote slipping out of your hand?

But needless to say, the long ride tires out the adults and the kids wake up with their energy packs teeming with fuel.

So we unleashed them on my parents—I mean, we opened the van doors and the children enthusiastically greeted their grandparents.

The kids had a blast picking tomatoes in the garden (the little ones ate all the green ones), playing computer games (the little ones poked their fingers in every outlet), running through the sprinklers (the little ones tried to play chicken with oncoming traffic), eating treats at the fair (the little ones complained because they were strapped in the stroller) and taking the dog for a walk (the little ones took themselves off for a walk unbeknown to the adults and thankfully went in the opposite direction of the busiest road).

Amid the joy of visiting, my husband and I were nervous wrecks as we pulled parental double-duty and *still* the little ones slipped through our fingers and under our radar and things were broken.

Nothing puts a damper on a visit than little ones who are quicker than the seven adults that are present.

That's when adults start looking at each other, pointing fingers and passing the buck. That's when the innocent run to the victim and beg for mercy: I didn't do it, he was in charge, we didn't see it coming, I wasn't even in the room....

I made up a list to help parents traveling and visiting with little ones:

1) Frequently poke the children when traveling to encourage them to stay awake. Invest in a spray bottle and use it.

2) Offer ample drinks when traveling. You may have to make more stops, but everybody stays awake.

3) Duct tape oven mitts to children under three. This prevents them from picking up miniature collectibles.

4) Bring a stake and leash for wandering toddlers. Stake the child in the backyard. She can run and play as she pleases, without slipping out the front door and down the street.

5) Wrap the clumsiest children in bubble wrap. This will protect the walls from dents when they forget and run through the house and then collide with inanimate objects.

6) Bring a playpen for children under the age of three to corral them when they just won't leave the untouchables alone. Use the above stake and leash for older children that do not stay out of rooms that are off limits.

7) Bring a whistle to get the attention of little ones feigning ignorance due to the large amount of people.

8) Bring an IV. This will prevent unnecessary spills.

9) Bring videos the children have not yet seen. Make that television babysitter work for you!

10) Bring plenty of aspirin. You'll need it.

With that said, we had a blast. The food was good and the company was even better. Hope your visits are just as wonderful.

Chapter Four

~Negotiations~

What Experts Call Parenting

Who Wants A Cookie?

Don't tell ME I'm teaching my kids how to deal with stress by eating. If you do, and I believe you, I'll lose my greatest strategy as a mom.

A mom can gauge the temperature of a situation not just by the number of wails and shrieks, but also by the penchant the kids have at any given time for lining up trouble, systematically, in rapid-fire succession.

It just seems like they reach a point where they no longer have the capacity to entertain themselves constructively and so they go at each other.

It's about that point, when I'm going after each child for the fifth time (I have five, remember) that, like a referee calling a time out, I stand straight and tall and announce loudly: WHO WANTS A

97

COOKIE?

Immediately, I have pleasant, eager children vying for my attention as I dole out the sweet crisp rounds I secretly call manna from heaven.

Yes, life is good when mom has cookies to share.

And you know, you get different responses with different types of cookies.

Say you were running tight on the grocery budget this month and you bought that really cheap barrel of animal crackers. You know, the kind that makes you feel just a tad less guilty for indulging your children because they are not *really* real cookies?

Well, the kids will take them—they take anything that's even remotely edible, they're like locusts—but nirvana only lasts for as long as it takes them to eat the animal crackers which is why I give them heaping handfuls of the things just to buy myself some more peaceful time.

Next on the list: Oreos. Yes, Oreos were made for milk. The E.N.T. (estimated nirvana time) for these treats is approximately the same amount of time it takes to dunk, chew and slop chocolate on the walls down the hall on the way to the bathroom to wash up...where they start bickering again. HOWEVER, if you usher your children out the door quickly enough the E.N.T increases three-fold. Thank God for sugar highs!

Finally, there are the HOMEMADE cookies. These are my secret weapons. I start baking them before the kids arrive home. It's an amazingly potent tactic. You can hear them clamoring up the walk. They hit the door and barrel through and then..?

Ahhhhhhhhhhhhh, *Mother*! You made COOKIES!!

Eager beavers quickly change into their play clothes and wash up. They savor each morsel of homemade cookie (chocolate chip is the best—it even works on my dear husband) and then, enchanted, they float to their rooms to happily complete their homework and chores and I get a gold star for the day.

Yeah, maybe it's bribery. Maybe it's not high on the child experts' lists of proper and healthy parenting. But I don't care.

My kids will remember the cookies when they look back on their childhoods as adults.

And maybe, just maybe, when the pressures of the world get to be a little too much, instead of turning to alcohol, drugs, inappropriate relationships or other addictions—*even* overeating—they'll just sit down and have a couple of cookies and a glass of milk.

Sounds good, doesn't it?

Who wants a cookie?

Why Do I Even Bother?

It popped out of my mouth this afternoon before I even gave it a second thought. And after eleven years of motherhood you'd think I'd have learned my lesson by now but, no. Thirty minutes before my husband is due home I announce: Time to pick up all the toys!

Yeah, right.

The three-year old applauded my efforts, but did she pitch in? Noooooo. In fact she feigned to not recall the words she already knows, words like "pick," "up" and "toys."

Any other time of the day you'll catch her PICK-ing her nose, climbing UP onto the sofa and strewing TOYS everywhere. The words work and make sense to her, except when Mom uses them altogether in a sentence, especially a sentence entailing some kind of WORK.

So, naturally, the two-year old follows me and picks up every toy. Hmmmmmmm.

"THANK YOU!" I tell him. "THANK yooooooooo!" he says back.

Hmmmmmmmm.

"Hey, Becca," I call to my three-year old, hoping she'll want to join in the 'fun' we're having. "Come help pick up toys!"

She looks at me with a lopsided grin and her eyes scrunched closed. Translation: "I don't know what you mean, Mom! Speaka da English!"

Sigh.

The baby and I get the living room picked up. All the toys are put away.

Along comes Becca, PICK-ing UP her TOYS and bringing them all back. "Wheeeeeeeeeeeeeee!" Oh, she's having some fun now!

But that just goes to show you that there must be a list of things moms say either because hope springs eternal, or we're losing our short-term memory little by little. These are things we say or ask and SHOULD know that we aren't going to get an answer to or any cooperation with, things that go in one ear and right out the other, yet we speak them anyway.

Things like:

> Time to pick up the toys.
> Who left the door open?
> Who left their underwear on the floor?
> Wash--with soap!

Did you brush your teeth?

Is your room picked up?

Are we mad?! Obviously, whatever we moms say sounds like one of those annoying mosquitoes that keep you up all night.

"Put your coat on before you go out to play!" translates to "Buzzz-buzzzy-buzzz-buzzz!"

For what it's worth, moms have some tricks up their sleeves. Take those sentences above and make a few substitutions. Speak in a soft voice. Any child within a hundred yards will come running— INSTANTLY.

For example, substitute, "Time to pick up the toys," with "Time to pick up a new video game." Substitute, "Who left the door open?" with "Who left this five dollar bill on the table?" Substitute, "Who left their underwear on the floor?" with, "Who wants a cookie?"

See what I mean? Toys, money and food all have POWER when it comes to negotiating—I mean talking with your kids.

That's why they love your parents so much. Grandma and Grandpa know what the power is and they use it. Oh, but they use it!

The kids whose attention you can't capture for more than five minutes at a time, the same kids that answer, 'Yeah, mom," to everything and go blithely on their way, the very kids you have to send a barrage of commands to before they begin to respond are the same kids that come running whenever Grandma and Grandpa come to visit.

Your mom says: "Now let's see what sort of cookies Grammy

has..."

Your dad says: "Now let's see if Grandpa has any extra dollars for the children..."

Kids come from all directions. They heard the magic words and phrases: "cookies," "money," and "for the children."

So what *can* we moms do?

Wait patiently until *we* are grandparents...and then have some fun!

Television 5, Mom 1

Hello! Earth to child!

It's no use talking to your kids when the television is on.

They try. They really do. You can see their heads turn slightly and their ears cock, but the eyes...they just keep trailing back to whatever is on the tube. Even the news!

Now my kids don't find that much interesting about the news, but when I need their attention suddenly it's the most magnetic thing in the universe. "Wow, Mom, the dow is up three quarters, did ya know that?"

Like with anything else that interests the children, I've got to compete.

So, I've been dressing like a Teletubby....

You know, having that television on my belly sure does the trick.

At least I have their eyes focused in my direction!

Then, I programmed some subliminal messages in what appeared to be mindless cartoons to the kids. Things like, "Pick up your clothes," "Eat your vegetables," "Finish your chores."

It must be working! You'd think Christmas was a mere few weeks away by the sight of my house. It's neat and clean and there are helpful children everywhere.

Seriously. Something is up around here. It's too soon for the Christmas rush on good behavior. And no one has ever thought to turn on the charm for Halloween, so naturally, whenever my kids do what I expect of them *without me asking*, I'm suspicious!

So now I'm going around the house looking for something that's been broken or lost or changed in some way. *Something* happened. It had to have! You just don't get five kids cooperating like this unless something is afoot!

It's enough to cause a small nervous breakdown in a mother after three or four unrelenting days of well-behaved children.

Aha! So *that's* the plan! They're doing this to drive me crazy! I *knew* they were up to something. And just because I've taken to talking to myself and I have this unrelenting facial tic doesn't mean they've won. No way. I'm on to them. I'm ready!

The sound of a dish breaking puts my heart to ease. The ensuing squabble over whose fault it is brings a smile to my lips. The rush to tattletale puts a gleam in my eye.

Ahhhhhhhh. It's good to have things back to normal again.

I turn on the television and the bickering dies down as all eyes turn to worship the great god of brain candy.

Television 5, Mom 2.

Time Outs Are Negative

I have a friend who is doing a great service in this world, one for which I greatly admire her and her husband. They are counselors for troubled youth and they live with up to a dozen boys that are troubled and in need of intervention.

Unfortunately, my friend has just moved to a new group home where the Mommy Cops (in close association with the Parenting Police--you know, the ones that stop you in the store and critique your parenting for free?) have invaded this particular group home community. The difference between the two is this: Parenting Police constantly find fault and critique with their crooked finger and pointy black shoes and hats, and Mommy Cops beam in with a sparkly magic wand and cheerfully correct your parenting with behavior modeling--you know, you feel like they are parenting you as they do it. Can you just see me rolling my eyes?

So my friend is now plagued by the Mommy Cops. For example, a child that threatens the adult in charge and hotwires a car and takes off should not have his privileges taken away. Missing out on television, dessert and phone calls from friends for two weeks (at least) would be demeaning. No kidding!

And let's not call a time out a time out. What should we call it? A time IN?

Time outs are negative. We talk with the child, explain why what he did is wrong and then it is over. Negative parenting, like suspending privileges, only prolongs the discomfort.

Really? I thought that was what parenting was all about--making our kids suffer as much as possible. But I digress.

Ordinarily, or should I say archaically, parenting was meant to be instructive. Discipline means to teach. My own dog doesn't get treats for doodling on the floor, I don't think a child that breaks a known rule with spelled out consequences should skip those consequences.

But isn't that the world we live in now? Every wrong done is simply an illness now that must be treated. Every mistake has a corresponding positive that must be accentuated. And my kids are smart enough to pick up on the concept.

"Have you finished your homework?"

"I did the best I could."

"Did you complete it?"

"I'm working on it."

"How much is done?"

"Most of it..." (That generally means the name, date, and possibly the first question.)

And that's another thing. You can't get a straight answer from kids these days. My daughter does a sloppy job washing dishes and she will insist that what matters is that she did SOME of them well enough. Yay, for self-esteem in education! Now, we have kids who do half as well just as good. Ahem.

So I stopped at my favorite burger joint to treat the kids the other day. We got cheeseburgers without the patty. I said what's this? The clerk said, but I gave you cheese and veggies....

And they were GOOD veggies, too! What was I complaining about?

I know. I forgot. I was negating his positive work experience by demanding a hamburger patty.

So I thought that instead of submitting a column with 700 words this week, I'd submit one with 350 words...and they were darn good words, I tell you.

But the editor didn't pay me for them. I said, "I ALMOST finished the column." She said she ALMOST renewed my contract.

That means I'm on a time out right now, doesn't it? Surely, I am not fired. That would be too negative and would prolong my discomfort. I'd have to sign up for counseling and then where would I be?

"It all started, Doctor, when I was in this group home and the new mother in charge took away my television and phone privileges and wouldn't let me have dessert for two weeks...."

Subliminal Parenting

I want to get my hands on some equipment so I can create videos for my kids to watch with subliminal messages.

Why not? What would happen if, while they watch their favorite cartoon, they suddenly get the urge to go clean up after themselves in the bathroom?

Okay maybe that is going overboard. If my kids got that urge, they'd quit watching TV. I don't blame them. So the plan is to go small, to be both subliminal and subtle.

I could splice in messages that suggest they share. Feel-good messages about how wonderful it is to share your toys with your siblings…instead of dangling them over the younger ones and making them cry and beg.

Here is a list of subliminal messages we could send the kids:

- Homework is best completed the night it is assigned, not five minutes before it is due.

- It's better to eat your veggies the first time, rather then stuffing them in between the leaves of the table.

- Shirtsleeves aren't napkins or tissues.

- Underwear and pants are separate items; please pull them apart before tossing in the hamper.

- "It's time to leave" means it's time to get in the car NOW, not go to the bathroom or search for your jacket.

- "It's time to eat" means that it's time to eat NOW, not go to the bathroom or read one more chapter of your favorite book

- "It's time for bed" means go to bed now, not start a homework assignment.

- "Advance notice" means give Mom a few days to prepare for your 4-H presentation/meeting/class party. Don't tell her five minutes before the event.

- "Thank you" and "Please" are definitely magic words and work on parents like a charm.

These must be every parent's dream, though I can see smart kids doing the same in return, adding subliminal messages like the following:

- Dessert will be served every night.

- There will be no chores on Saturday.

- Allowances will be increased 500%.

- Television viewing will be increased to four hours a night.

- X-Box games will be played BEFORE homework.

- The only vegetables served will be corn-on-the-cob and French fries.

- I never have to help change a stinky diaper again.

- No little brothers or sisters will be allowed in my room again.

When it comes down to it, there are probably a million subliminal messages kids and parents would like to exchange to make family life more idyllic, but the best of all (and it doesn't have to be said covertly) is "I love you."

Glass of Water For A Drowning Mom

My son is a big complainer when it comes to folding laundry. He's only eight, but I think he's capable AND this will be a good skill for him as an adult.

Nevertheless, I am constantly thinking of new ways to present this daily chore without his getting into histrionics. Recently, I called him to my room and showed him my five heaping baskets of clothes. His eyes bugged out. I asked him if he would like to fold these or his own. He very cheerfully volunteered to do his own.

But being the stickler he is for 'fairness' he soon returned with half a basket full of clothes. "These are not mine," he informed me.

From the center of the mounds of towels I was folding, I asked him if he could fold the extra clothes anyway.

He stood his ground. "They aren't mine."

So I tried a mother's favorite weapon: guilt. "Fine. Thanks for letting me know I can't count on you."

He didn't even crack.

So, I tried philosophy. "Son, if I were drowning in a lake, would you give me a glass of water?"

"What?"

"If I were drowning, would you give me water?"

"Oh," he said, and left the room with me feeling rather smug. I'd successfully avoided a heated confrontation with philosophy! Who says stay-at-home-moms don't use their college education? I congratulated myself on how smart I am and how smart my kids are. And while I was glowing with these thoughts, my son returned...with a glass of water. He had a gleam in his eye, too.

And that's how it is with kids. You have to possess the faculties of a lawyer just to stay one step ahead of these munchkins. When you succeed, you gloat and enjoy the moment, because you're going to fail the next seven moments in a row.

For instance, while I was folding clothes I heard the sound of the lid on the cookie jar being removed. "Who's in the cookie jar?" I yelled down the hall.

"Nobody!"

"Who is nobody?"

"Nicole."

I called her to my room, where I was still trying to climb out from the well of clothes I was folding. "What are you doing in the cookie jar?"

"Counting them." Suddenly, the nobody that was doing nothing in the cookie jar was taking a census. Do I look stupid or what? Don't answer that.

"Nicole, that is the worst attempt at lying I have ever heard."

"But I'm not lying."

"That's another lie and if you keep this up," I warned, "you might end up being President of the United States someday."

Meanwhile, my son returns with a glass of milk.

"What is this for?"

"You said you can't drink water if you're drowning," he says with a further gleam in his eye.

Riiiiiiiiiiiiiiiight. My kids are so bright they know how to feign stupidity. Just hand me another glass of water. It makes perfect sense to me.

House Full of Sorry Heads

Yesterday there wasn't a child alive in our house that wasn't looking hang-dogged and pitiful. From the eldest to the youngest, somebody was in trouble.

It never fails to amaze me. As parents we want to share things with our kids, we want to reward them and create those memories that will one day be the 'good old days' and yet they have to go and pull some bone-headed thing and make you be the parent and not their friend.

The nerve.

And yet, when I think back on my own childhood, I can see a multitude of acts I committed that assured my parents that I had brain damage. I'm responsible for their bent backs, graying hair and crooked pointy fingers. Here is a Top Fifteen List (in no particular order) of the

117

things kids do that try their poor parents.

#1. They descend like locusts on whatever groceries you bring into the house and they squabble over a fair division. Fair my foot. My groceries are supposed to split seven ways and then some…so how come it only covers the five kids?

#2. The oldest have to push the buttons of the youngest just to hear the youngest squeal like a stuck pig. And then, just before you catch on, they comfort their victim and prep him for the next wave of teasing.

#3. Everybody is always starving. Yet the minute you set dinner on the table nobody is hungry and it takes them an hour and a half to finish a meal.

#4. Ida Know and Who Me are the names of the two other children you didn't know you had.

#5. Cats are made of rubber and are thus amazing contortionists in the hands of a two-year old.

#6. Your creative child tries to explain that she cut a miniature doll-sized hole in the bedroom wall so the fairies that live in the wall can come and go more freely.

#7. Milk evaporates at the speed of light and there is never more than a drop left in the carton in the fridge. Especially when you need some for a recipe…or for the baby's bottle.

#8. Time flies when it's time to do homework, but when it's time for bed, the moment stretches on for an eternity.

#9. Your honor roll students are the brightest in their grade, but you wouldn't know it at home because they leave their common sense in their desks at school.

#10. The child that speaks like a squeaky screen door is ALWAYS the child that talks to you the most.

#11. They don't actually WEAR the clothes, but somehow they get soiled and end up in the hamper just the same. There's nothing like washing every article of clothing of every child every week.

#12. They all clamor to 'go for a ride' when you're going to the store, you take them, and then you wonder WHY.

#13. Since no one in your house smokes, your eight-year old takes it upon himself to evangelize the neighborhood by harassing neighbors with his memorized statistics on how smoking kills. Thank you, enlightened media.

#14. The cats want to eat the dog's food and the dog wants to eat the cats' food. That's not possible, so nobody is eating. (Hey, pets are kids, too!)

#15. Chewing gum makes a most excellent and permanent necklace.

And here is a list of five 'Need I say more?' situations. You've probably done these yourself as a kid.

#1. Scissors, girls, Barbie dolls, beauty school.

#2. Crayons, pockets, dryer.

#3. Older sibling, closet, youngster terrified of the dark.

#4. Kids, peanut butter, dog.

#5 Older sibling, cookie jar, younger child as lookout.

This is why parents can't be friends with their children. *Somebody* needs to keep order and yet it is precisely that which makes kids feel secure and happy. This creates the memories that will be the 'good old days.'

Please Say Please

I'm inflicting great hardship on my two-year old son. I want him to say 'please.' He'd rather point and bark out orders. "Get me my chocolate milk, wench!"

Well, who died and left him lord of the realm?

"Say pleeease."

"You. Get. Chocolate. Milk. NOW."

Obviously he fears my authority and is always more than willing to comply. I try to pry his sticky fingers from my calf because he has thrown himself at my feet and is endeavoring to control me by cutting off the blood to my varicose veins.

What's a mom to do? Shrug and drag my leg behind me as I make my way to his room. Suddenly, he is up and running full speed in the opposite direction. "No time out! NO TIME OUT!!"

While I am wrangling him back to his room, it occurs to me that none of the classes I took in high school or college prepared me for this. What good is Shakespeare now? Who cares what the purpose of an imaginary number is? The only writing around here is on the wall and it's a far cry from a sonnet. The only imaginary numbers I count daily are the cookies I think are still in the cookie jar. But they're not. And I should know better, but I keep looking in the cookie jar as if it will suddenly refill itself.

Silly me.

I think my two-year old son and I have a lot in common. We both demand that the other does what we want NOW. We'd both rather eat cookies all morning long instead of doing chores…and why not? All the other kids are in school. They'd be scandalized if they knew and a bit envious.

So I try to negotiate with him. BIG MISTAKE. The Mother's Manual says: NEVER negotiate with a hostage-taker. Yes, he is a hostage-taker. He snatched my sanity when I wasn't looking and he stuffed it in the crevice between the wall and his mattress, somewhere under a goobery, well-loved toy dog. I've been trying to get it back for months.

"NO!"

"PLEASE. Give Mommy back her sanity. Please?"

"NO!"

Why THAT word? I know he's asserting himself and becoming a more independent twerp, but why "NO!"? Why not "YES!"?

Because that would be too easy. Too positive. Too harmonious. And we can't have that.

I'd even settle for: "Maybe!" But no such luck.

So, I broke the rules and 'negotiated.' "If you want milk you need to say 'please.'"

"MILK!"

"Say 'please.'"

"APPLE!"

"Please."

"CARROT!"

"Please?"

"SANDWICH!"

"Please…?"

Big grin. "COOKIE PLEASE!"

I just HAD to give it to him.

Chapter Five

~Going Over The Edge~

Nailing The Door Shut On The Padded Room

Children, Television & Video Games

I'll give you three guesses as to why these sounds drive me nuts. If you guessed because they sound like A) children, B) television and C) video games, you're right!

I don't know about you, but I can't tell the difference between these three sounds and generally they tend to be background noise while I go about my daily business. Which is why I tend to panic when everything suddenly goes silent. Power outages I can handle, but the kids never lose power, they just have it surge elsewhere and that usually means trouble.

I was in my room the other day—Sunday—my day to take it a bit slower and sit down and read or write, when the voices of my eleven-year old daughters drifted in from their room across the hall from mine. "Babble bibble bobble babble babble boo," ad nauseum. I actually got up and went into the living room. If it's going to sound like cartoon chatter I may as well sit in front of the television.

But, no, there is my eight-year old son who, upon seeing me sit down to write quietly, decides that I need a second-by-second description of his every action. Why he does this, I don't know. I know I should be thankful because there will come a time when he WON'T tell me about what is happening in his life. But do I need to know it in such excruciatingly painful detail?

"Mom, look. This piece of my transforming robot moves up like this."

"Mom, look. This piece of my transforming robot moves sideways like this."

"Mom, look. This piece of my transforming robot moves down like this."

"Mom, look—"

"ALL RIGHT ALREADY!!!!"

Everyone stops and looks at me. I'm moulting. I've got pinfeathers. My eyes are turning in slow multi-colored spirals. I've got this manic grin, a facial tic, and I swear I could lay an egg if just one more child pushes me over the edge.

"Mom, look. This piece of my transforming robot moves—"

"AAAAAAAAAGGGGGGGGGGGHHHHHHHHH!!!"

"Bibble babble bobble boo!"

"AAAAGGGHHH! AAAAGGGGHHH! AAAAGGGHHH!"

"Hey, look, Mom just laid an egg! How did she do that? I didn't know Momma could lay eggs? Did we eat your eggs this morning, Momma, or did they come from the store? Look, Mom, when I move your egg like this it—"

"Puh-COCK!   Cluckcluckcluckcluckcluck-CLUCK!"   Does anybody even NOTICE that I can't take any more of this?? Does anybody care??

Why is it that when a mom finally gets down to her last nerve, everyone has the audacity to look surprised? Haven't they seen it coming?

Noooooooooo. Ask a stupid question.

"So, Mom, am I a chicken, too? Did I hatch from an egg?"

If chickens could deliver deadpan looks, I would.

What is it with kids and their endless questions? Okay, at first it was cute. And then it was a sign of intelligence. Now I wish they'd all get a good case of laryngitis.

So my husband and I are planning to run away…as soon as possible! He just doesn't know it yet. HE thinks he's going to work tomorrow. But I'm kidnapping him, commandeering a domestic flight and we're going to some faraway quiet place where no one is ever allowed to ask "Why?" again.

When they raise the terror alert to red, don't worry. It's not Osama, it's just one mad momma looking for a little peace and quiet.

Kid Magnets

I can't get my kids' attention to save my life. I could literally set myself on fire and dance in front of the television and they'd all tip to their left to see around me.

YET...let me pick up that phone and BAM! Five kids have the most urgent messages for me. There's nothing like trying to hold a conversation with somebody tugging on your sleeve and launching into a five minute monologue at the exact same decibel as the person on the line. If it's somebody important, you cover the mouthpiece and whisper harshly: "Go away! Later!"

But if it's your husband or your sister, you pepper your conversation with: "I'M ON THE PHONE! GET DOWN FROM THERE! WHO LET THE BABY EAT THE DOGFOOD?!"

Here's another kid magnet: A good book. Open up ANY book

and get interested and somebody is petting your arm or shoulder. "Mom, mom, mom, mom, mom, mom."

"What?"

"Uhhhh."

What, they can't remember longer than ten seconds? So you go back to reading.

"MOM!"

"What!"

"Uhhhh."

How about the bathroom? Nobody cares about me until I want a little privacy. Then, it's: "Can I have a snack?"

"Do you think I have anything in here you'd like to sample?"

"How long are you going to be?"

"As long as it takes!" Little do they know that at the push of a button the bathroom morphs into a private mom spa complete with a chocolate buffet and fan waving slaves. Or do they?

How about when you're trying to pay the bills? "600 take away 50...."

"Mom, I have something for you."

"Equals 450...plus 50 equals...."

"Mom, did you say we could have three cookies or five because John Daniel took six cookies."

"500? No, 450. What!?!"

"Six, he took six!"

"650? Hey, honey did you know we're fifty dollars ahead this week?"

The all time greatest kid magnet is when you get a few moments to talk to your dear husband and suddenly a head pops up between you. "I'm sorry, is the fact that your father and I are having a conversation bothering you?"

So I've learned a few tricks.

When conversing on the phone and a child comes within range, say: "Yes, I think the curriculum for the military academy is quite excellent and I'm sure my child could definitely benefit from it."

When heading for the bathroom, grab cleaning supplies. Nobody ever wants to help mom scrub the toilet. Then, ditch those items once you close the door.

Create a book cover titled "101 Chores When Your Kids Have Nothing Better To Do." Slip it on your favorite novel and enjoy.

When paying the bills place a tip jar on the table. They can give up part of their allowance if they REALLY have to talk to you. If your children don't have an allowance, this might be a good reason to give them one!

When talking with your husband, give him a smooch when children get in range. This almost always clears the room!

But, don't worry. None of these ideas will keep your children away indefinitely. Eventually they will want to eat, or be chauffeured somewhere or need their clothes washed. Mom, you're invaluable.

Don't you just love it?

Being A Parent Means No Time For Tears

It was the scream of a man that had just lost a limb, so I came running. Visions of my husband lying in a pool of blood, mortally wounded, came to mind. But it was worse than I had thought.

Our two-year old had twisted off the earpiece to my husband's Ray Bans.

I quickly whisked our tot away and stowed him safely in his room while my husband paced. He was so angry he wasn't going to speak to our son until he was old enough to sue for damages. It wasn't the opportune time to point out to my husband that it was pretty moronic of him to leave his very expensive birthday gift on the kitchen table like that. We have 'under-fours' in our house. That means that anybody that leaves anything lying within the reach of those under the age of four has officially abandoned the item to a hellish destruction.

And so my husband brooded. He wouldn't even look at the poor culprit until it was pretty evident that life goes on and a dad MUST exercise the law in the house. For it wasn't long before the little sunglass-wrecker was the life of the party at our dinner table, burping on command and warming up to start a good old-fashioned food fight with his older brother and sisters who, naturally, were encouraging him.

And that's how it is for parents. No matter what the little twerplets do, you can't nurse your bruised ego for very long at all, not unless you want to concede your high-ranking position in the household.

They strike quickly and then counterstrike so fast you lose all your short-term memory. As you sort through your confusion, all chaos breaks loose, and you wonder why you even let the little buggers into the world in the first place. These are the creatures we once called bundles of joy?!

For nine months you carried them worrying about every little development. And all you asked for was a healthy child with ten fingers and ten toes. And that is EXACTLY what you got.

You thought it would be too much to ask for anything more. You didn't want to wear out God's patience. Just give us a healthy child...and He did!

Just try to remember that while they are running through the house at breakneck speed chasing the terrified dog with the helium balloon tied to his tail. Keep your thankfulness in mind when you walk into what looks like a nuclear disaster in your kitchen when they've made you a birthday breakfast. And when they grab your sunglasses and twist them into pretzels remember with utter gratitude that they did that with those wonderful fingers you prayed for them to have.

It's been on the tip of my tongue to remind my husband that it was intelligence and curiosity that drove our son to unintentionally ruin his sunglasses. But I don't think he'd listen. He's too close to the source. Much like I am 24/7, it seems, when they run rampant in the house like a swarm of locusts, landing on project after project, finished chore after finished chore, and craft after craft of mine and just demolish them one by one.

I did the only thing I could do. I sent the kids to bed early and my husband and I enjoyed the quiet and a bowl of ice cream while we planned our escape, ah, I mean golden years.

There's a reason why grandparents love their grandbabies so much. It's because they see how much trouble and pain they are giving their parents. And it brings tears of joy to their eyes.

We plan on being such grandparents and we wish abundant blessings on our children, too.

The Mother of All Complaints

What is it with my kids and their instantaneous whine and litany of complaints the minute I walk in the room?

I was sitting on the floor behind the kitchen cabinets enjoying an ice cream cone after dinner. Yes, I have to do this because if the toddlers find out I have a treat when they don't (because they didn't eat their dinner) I will get nothing but "Me, me, me, me, meee!" and chubby little hands outstretched for my dessert. A mom just has to hide if she wants any peace when she indulges.

Anyway, I'm sitting out there among the cats—I have nine and can't get away from chubby little paws—and I'm listening to my little ones playing and having a grand old time. No whining.

Yet, the minute I go back into the main room, it's a litany of complaints. Diapers need changing, thirst needs quenching, hunger needs staving, the cat scratched me, my brother stole my Weeble, my sister took my car…. All this they save up for ME? Why not dad?

I'll tell you why. Dad doesn't give a care. And the kids know it. His justice is swift and final. "No car? Too bad. Go find something else to do." "Pants wet? Go get a diaper." "Hungry? You should have eaten your dinner." So they don't even bother with dad. And they're HAPPY.

The minute I walk in the room they come undone like they've barely managed to breathe the entire time I was gone. And I'm dumb enough to try to resolve the problem. But that never works. Take the car they were fighting over, for example. The minute you take the car from one, the other throws herself on the floor in a livid fit. "My car! My car! My car! My car!"

That's when parents make judgments that aren't logical they're just necessary. You find yourself saying something brilliant like: There will be NO MORE toy cars in this house and that's final!

Like that will ever happen. I have two boys with enough Matchbox cars to cause a major gridlock in our hallway. This is when my husband gives me that look, the one that lets me know he's the superior parent.

But I boldly try to work out the dilemma. Have you ever tried to convince a screaming toddler that the BLUE car is just as good as the RED car? How about the blue car, the green car, the yellow truck and a cookie? Ah, that works! Now we're negotiating!

My husband reminds me that they didn't eat their dinner. Is it really necessary? Cookies have wheat in them and eggs and raisins. All they need is milk! Look, it's four of the major food groups!

Give me a break. And isn't it their bedtime anyway? You mean they HAVE to stay up until eight? Is that a law? Can't we just start bedtime at noon?

I'd file a complaint but there's no one in that department except me. Time to make a phone call: "Hi, Mom, it's me. Waaaaaah!"

Out of the Mouths of Parents

You know you're at the end of your rope when you find yourself issuing decrees to your children that no person in their right mind in this modern age should do. Decrees such as the one my husband uttered recently.

Our eight-year old had taken a small step backward in his personal cleanliness. It's bound to happen, but some days it staggers the mind. This weekend's example was my husband's discovery of the boy's very used underwear hanging on the knob of another child's dresser drawer.

This is on the heels of his personal hygiene taking a real dive. No soap in the shower, no brushing teeth, wearing the same clothes too many times without a wash, etc.

So my husband made our son wear his underwear on his head

for an hour to make sure the next time he was tempted to be so lazy he'd resist. And my husband decreed: "Let this be a lesson to you...to not hang your underwear on other people's... *knobs.*

I could tell my husband was fumbling there at the end and it was all I could do to shut myself in the dryer so he wouldn't hear me laughing—as you do when you're not the parent on duty and you're enjoying listening to your spouse wrangle with the twerplets.

To make matters worse (for me) he went on: "You're a gnat's testicle away from turning nine-years old and you should know better!"

Now I have never thought much of gnats, let alone their private matters, but the whole thing struck me as hysterical and so I had to turn the dryer on to muffle my own amusement.

Whereupon my husband asks me just what I think I'm doing and have I lost my mind. (I was also a gnat's testicle away from my own birthday. Perhaps these incidences are all birthday related.) I responded with an oldie but a goodie—one I've learned from my kids: "I don't know!"

So now it's a race to see which one of us, my husband or I, turns old and gray first. I'm thinking he's going to beat me because he doesn't do near as much to astound me as I do him.

Whenever he asks the kids a rhetorical question, I'm the first to answer. And how many times does the poor man ask the kids just what in the blazes do they think they are doing just to learn that mom said they could? Why CAN'T you have dessert before dinner every once in awhile? Who said you had to color inside the lines when you can color all over the driveway, sidewalk and street with chalk?

Dr. Laura says that parents balance each other out. Her example was the rough and tumble father and the nurturing mom. In our house it's sometimes the follow-the-rules dad and the don't-be-afraid-to-show-your-doofiness mom. Except I do it all by accident.

Which reminds me of a great quote I read once: "They say I have ADD. I don't think so. Hey, look at that cat!"

My husband was talking to the neighbor the other day getting advice on how to fix our plumbing problems. While we are all standing on the lawn to discuss this like reasonable adults, our cat runs by and I chase him. So we are middle-aged. Does that mean life is to be lived predictably?

At least I don't hang my underwear on other people's knobs. My husband should be grateful. He's just a gnat's testicle away from going insane, too.

The Bad Hair Day

The house is filled with flies again—I can't stand it. It gets that way when the weather turns hot. There are horses just a block away from us and all the flies seem to congregate at my house. Small town living, big time flies.

One year I hung up flypaper in the corners of the kitchen. It didn't work. All the flies circled in the center. So I tried swinging the flypaper through the 'fly-cloud,' and ended up with the stuff stuck to my arm: very gooey and not easily removed with soap and water. A fine example of sheer brilliance on my part.

I finally moved the flypaper to the center of the kitchen and it worked! At long last I was catching flies and dancing a victory dance…but it was much to premature for that.

Now, I usually wear my hair up in this fuzzy feather duster style.

It suits my busy life chasing kids and cats and running from one project to another, which is exactly what I was doing that hot autumn day.

And sure enough, as I bustled through the kitchen with the baby on my hip, I got too close to the flypaper. It totally stuck to my head, especially the fuzzy duster hairdo, and plastered to my bangs. The more I pulled, the more stuck I got and the more flypaper rolls I managed to stick to my head—all said I had three rolls completely wrapped in my hair. Worse, I had all these dead and dismembered flies buzzing in my ears and mere centimeters from my eyes and mouth.

Police investigators later recorded my children's statements as they tried to piece together the event.

"Her eyes rolled back in her head and she screamed like one of our cats when they get in a fight. We thought we were in big trouble!"

"Then Momma ran through the house—with SCISSORS in her hands!"

Yes, I did, and but for the grace of God I did not clip myself bald. It's a miracle my new hairdo turned out as nicely as it did.

So this year I'm really trying to master the Zen of living with flies. No, I can't catch them with chopsticks, but I'm picking and choosing my battles. Still, the stress builds up.

Ever notice how violent a person can get when it comes to flies? You can tell how long they have put up with the buggers by the way they go after them.

I used to work as an aide in a class for severely emotionally disturbed children. It was during one of the staff meetings that this truth was so perfectly illustrated.

Therapist (in a calm voice while a fly buzzes lazily around him and he passively waves his hand): "We need to model patience and peace to these children. (He waves in annoyance and the faintest facial tic emerges.) But at the same time we have to gently, but firmly lead them... (more buzzing, a sudden fierce swipe) like Ms. Annie did with Helen Keller (buzz) DANG FLIES!!!" He grabbed a baseball bat and we all ran for the car.

It's amazing how God's smallest creatures can antagonize us.... Oh, yeah. That's why I write this column.

The Agony of Raising Children

That which does not kill us makes us stronger.

If my three-year old daughter doesn't kill me with her temper tantrums I am going to be MRS. UNIVERSE!

Friday she lit into one five-hour long rage. Rolling around on her bedroom floor, kicking her feet, screaming and yelling. All this because I asked her to take a time out in her room for five minutes...for what, though, I cannot remember. I fear my memory has been erased.

Just like when you put a floppy disk on top of the computer or on the microwave, this ill-tempered child had drained all of the content of my brain.

By the time my eight-year old son returned home from school, I was completely on edge. "DON'T start with me," I warned him, as he slid easily into HIS whining and stomping and fit throwing. I don't even remember what that was about. I just know it was another child screaming.

"I'M A MOMMA ON THE EDGE!" I warned, again.

There's something about being a child—and I remember this well from my own childhood—that causes these vertically challenged love dumplings to just blow right past the caution and yield signs and take a mom right over the edge.

PMS has nothing on a mom when she goes over the edge.

It starts with a glaring squint and a deep frown. Then the right hand deforms into this crooked pointy finger and the voice turns abrasive and wickedly witchy. "I TOLLLLLD YOU NOT TO STARRRRT WITH MEEEEEEEEEE!"

And they always have the NERVE to look surprised!

Mom was patient. Mom warned them. Mom gave them choices and opportunities to do something that would keep everything on an even keel, but no! They go for the brass ring. They utter their own squeaky shrill demands. They defy the very edge of the nervous breakdown you are teetering on and they give you that one last nudge that sends you over the edge.

While my daughter continued her tirade in her room, my son saw it as an opportunity to work things in his favor. I'd sent him to his room and had issued the decree that if he did not follow directions he'd spend the rest of his life in his room…to which he calmly replied: "I don't know if I can trust you."

In the hurricane of my madness, in the eye of the storm, I

stopped and looked down at this child who met my eyes plainly as if he had spoken the golden truth and now held some sort of power over me.

Very succinctly, I said, "What. Did. You. Say?"

Without any sign of fear he calmly stated, "I said, I don't know if I can trust you."

Curiousity got the best of me. "You don't know if you can trust me about WHAT?"

"I don't know if I can trust that you love me."

You know, sometimes I have to secretly admire my kids for being little smarties. Even though this was sheer manipulation and a bit of defiance, I had to admit he showed great intelligence by choosing and working that angle. NOT!

I read him the riot act: "Nice try! For your information, love is a LOT MORE than presents for no reason at all, trips to fun and exciting places and whatever you want to eat whenever." (He was preparing for a weekend with his dad, my ex.) "My love as a parent is making rules and holding you to them and helping you live in such a way that you grow up to be a happy and productive adult. Those other things are nice, but without rules it's just sugar and it can spoil you rotten."

Of course I left the room feeling like HE'D won, but I left with my shoulders squared and my finger crooked so he wouldn't KNOW it.

Apparently, I am a less-than parent because our home isn't orchestrated like Circus Circus for the kids.

1. I don't plan entertaining and engaging activities for them every

hour or afternoon they are home.

2. I don't have special outings planned. I simply go to the store, go to the bank, go to the doctor and go to church.

3. I make one meal and expect everyone to eat it or not.

4. We have house rules and we expect them to be followed. When they aren't followed there are consequences.

5. I don't buy toys or things at the drop of a hat. I have to budget for them.

That's not to say that we don't do things as a family and that we never have fun. It's just that our fun is spread over a long period of time. In between those events is something we call LIFE and FAMILY. I have to stress to this child in particular that he is NOT a GUEST in this home. He is a FAMILY MEMBER.

We didn't have any more problems the rest of the day and my daughter finally gave up and settled into her happy self again.

But I tell you it took me three days to finish wowing over my son's attempt to manipulate. Ooh, they're making these newest kid models trickier!

Chapter Six

~Mental & Physical Health~

Last But Not Least

A Mom's New Year's Resolution

This year I resolve to...

1)   Leave the house on time and keep all my appointments. **Flashback:** Mom in the van revving the engine, hollering out the window as three kids hop to the van pulling on their shoes, "You better be in this van by the time I count to three or I'm leaving you in the dust!

2)   Make nutritious dinners that nurture the family as well as nourish them. **Flashback:** Kids wrinkling noses at spinach salad and broiled fish and mom saying, "You eat what I cook—it cost me money!

3)   Support my kids at the school in all their activities. **Flashback:** Mom on the sidelines shaking her fist and arguing with the referee while the kids melt away,

mortified. "What do you mean that's out of bounds, what are you, a moron?!"

4) Take my kids to the museum and expose them to culture. **Flashback:** Tiny tot pointing at David's 'appendage' clinically labeling it at high volume and explaining to all within earshot what the difference is between boys and girls.

5) Lead my family in good health and fitness. **Flashback:** Attempting to power walk down the sidewalk while three-year old runs toward street and two-year old runs through gardens.

6) Plan fun and interesting family outings. **Flashback:** Family packed in van with the baby crying non-stop for thirty miles. One wants a drink, another has to go to the bathroom and the third is going to be sick. "Are we there yet!?"

7) Teach kids about their heritage and family. **Flashback:** Aunt Helda pinching the littlest one's cheeks and the oldest child making faces and crying out, "Ack! She smells old! Do I have to kiss her?"

8) Be a cool mom and let kids have more sleepovers. **Flashback:** Lying in bed at three o'clock in the morning while a chorus of pre-teen girls giggle all through the night.

9) Make sure all cats have clean bill of health.

Flashback: Curtains torn to shreds, artery on left wrist slashed, cat wrapped in a towel with bugged-out eyes spitting out wormer pill for the fourth time in a row.

10) Make more time for myself. **Flashback:** Soaking in the tub by candlelight while kids line up to pound on door. "Are you done yet, Mom? What are you doing in there? I think she's asleep. Are you asleep, Mom? Want me to get Dad? I smell something burning. Maybe we should call the fire department."

11) Eat fewer sweets. **Flashback:** There was Johnny's birthday party at school, the reception after Sally's dance recital, Halloween, Christmas, Valentine's, St. Patrick's Day....

12) Teach the toddlers more words and prepare them for preschool and kindergarten. **Flashback:** Telling off the idiot that backed into me at a stop light only to have the little ones share the 'new' words they learned when they greeted the minister at church the following Sunday.

Hmmmm. Maybe I'll just tear up this list and have a little chocolate from my stash. This resolution business is for the birds.

Senior Moments

I'll tell you what a senior moment is. It's standing at the refrigerator filling up a glass at the water dispenser and forgetting what it was I came in the kitchen to do. Yes, seriously, that was me the other night. I'm standing there, gazing around the room trying to puzzle out what it was that I came into the kitchen to do and then caught myself in time before the glass overflowed. How can a person forget what they are doing while they are doing it!?!? The kids are sucking the life from me, I swear.

I told them all to give me hugs and love before I forget who they are. I don't know if I should be worried. They looked alarmed like I'd spoken out loud what everybody has already been thinking.

Good grief I'm only thirty-six. Is this the beginning of my senior years? Already?

Is that why I'm ready for bed right after dinner and then I'm up at the crack of dawn? Is this why I keep trying to make the kids take a nap, so I can, too? "But, Mom, I'm in MIDDLE SCHOOL."

And yet I have to wait another fourteen years before I qualify for A.A.R.P.

I could be a long lost missing person by then. I can just see it. One day I go to the grocery store, by myself, and then next thing I know I'm in Indiana. I live in California.

So I am taking some pre-cautions to stave off the onset of my senior years or to at least fake it so nobody else knows my state of mind.

1. I'm taking at least one kid with me no matter where I go. That way I have somebody to remind me what I came for and tell me how to get back home.

2. I'm learning to nod and smile when people speak to me (my hearing is going, too). But mostly, once I get three sentences into a conversation with another adult, I can't remember what we were talking about in the first place.

3. I'm taking ginkgo-balboa a herb that increases memory…just as soon as I remember where I put the bottle.

4. I'm taking a proactive stance and I've made up business cards that say: I'm lost. Please call my husband at ###-####…but I need to remember where I put those, also.

5. I'm getting the OnStar system installed in my van. Maybe THEY know where I live.

6. I started taping notes all over the house so I remember really important things…like picking up my husband at work when I have the car for the day.

One night I went for a walk and I was SURE this car was following me; the driver flashed his lights at me. I tried not to panic and I stepped up my pace. By the time I broke into a full run, the car had caught up to me…and my husband yelled out: "What do you think you're doing?!"

That's another thing. My husband and I have been having these arguments over silly things. He asks me where such and such is and I walk out of the room. He finds me standing in another room staring blankly at the wall.

"Why did you walk out on me like that?"

"Didn't you ask for such and such?"

"I did; is it in this room?"

"Is what in this room?" (See? Three sentences in….)

"The such and such!"

"We have one of those? Where is it?"

"That's what I asked you!"

It's really annoying. Maybe I should ask my doctor if this is a side effect from one of the medications I take. I'm sure he can be of help…. What was I talking about?

Twelve Steps For Parents

1. **We admitted we were powerless over our children – that our lives had become unmanageable.** We could not manage to get them to eat their peas, pickup after themselves, share with their siblings, complete their chores and not wait until the last moment to tell us about the cupcakes we were supposed to bake for their class.

2. **We came to believe that a power greater than ourselves could restore us to sanity.** So we called our parents and asked THEM to take the kids for the weekend.

3. **We made a decision to turn our will and our lives over to the care of God as we understood God.** We threw our hands up in the air and cried: God help us all!

157

4.	**We made a searching and fearless inventory of ourselves**…and discovered that our parents' curse was working. Our kids were behaving just as we had when we were children!

5.	**We admitted to ourselves and to another human being the exact nature of our wrongs…** We informed our spouse that it was his/her fault for being so romantic in the first place.

6.	**We were entirely ready to remove these defects of character.** Again, we tried to send the kids to Grandma's house….

7.	**We humbly asked to remove our shortcomings.** Grandma was no longer answering the phone for some mysterious reason…so we called Auntie Jenn and asked if SHE would like to have the kids for the weekend.

8.	**We made a list of all persons we had harmed, and became willing to make amends to them all.** We offered to PAY Grandma, Auntie Jenn or ANYBODY to take the kids if even for just a couple of hours!

9.	**We made direct amends to such people wherever possible, except when to do so would injure them or others.** Finding that no relative could be bribed, we planned a trip to Disneyland for the family

158

instead.

10.   **We continued to take personal inventory and when we were wrong promptly admitted it**. Again we informed our spouse that it was his/her fault for being so romantic in the first place…but that it was okay because a family vacation was just what we needed.

11.   **We sought to improve ourselves and find the power to carry that out**. We discovered that Disneyland is a lot bigger than it first appeared and we prayed for the stamina to keep up with the kids!

12.   **Having had a spiritual awakening as the result of these steps…**we decided that one more addition to the family wouldn't kill us…and we made the most of the weekend while the older kids chaperoned the younger kids on our family vacation.

An Untimely Terrible Infection

I got this Untimely Terrible Infection a few weeks ago. And like a brave mom, I tried to take care of my malady at home, quietly, instead of with a quick trip to the doctor's office. I drank gallons of cranberry juice and water and gained ten pounds but that didn't save my kidneys from the spread of the Untimely Terrible Infection.

And wouldn't you know it? My toddlers could all sense my pain...and they did their best to maximize it.

The three-year old kept jumping on the sofa jostling my poor throbbing kidneys. Every time I tried to sit somewhere more stable, the two-year old would climb up behind me and plant his feet firmly on either side of my lower spine.

How do kids know? My aches and pains are like a kid magnet!

It's like having a sunburn on your back and suddenly everybody

160

you know is patting it.

Or having a blister on your toe and kids keep stepping on your feet. I could stand on hot coals and fare better than I would around my children.

Why do moms put off caring for themselves? Why do we put off going to the doctor? Do we have some kind of martyr gene?

We are often the last ones on our list of people to care for or think of. Just check out your holiday gift-giving list the next time you write one. There's the grill for your husband, the books for your kids, cookies for every neighbor and acquaintance you ever made, not to mention cards to over 200 people you're not sure you could even recognize on the street.

But where's the little something for Mom?

Look at Dad's list. He's buying Mom a new table saw. He is giving her the gift of him building her a patio enclosure. That's pretty shrewd. Last year he gave her lumber so he could build her a greenhouse.

Likewise, Mom COULD give Dad the gift of a slinky negligee— and sometimes she does—but the truly SELFISH for-mom-ONLY present? What is that?

You begin to think about that when your kidneys are throbbing. For me those are organs just a bit too close to the area of my body that ached and carried these children for nine months. Somewhere along the line, those happy bundles of joy stole our two-hour bubble baths from us. And how many Moms have you heard utter, "What's a novel?"

So, while I was sitting there in my misery with this Untimely Terrible Infection, I thought about my self. It was time to do a little pampering. So I bought the pair of ceramic chickens at the thrift store that I'd been keeping my eye on. Of course, like a true mom, I made sure they were sale items discounted at fifty percent.

I also bought a pint of sorbet and, you guessed it, as soon as I walked in the door there were kid eyes trained on my package, completely oblivious to my Untimely Terrible Infection.

Of course I shared. I am a mom, after all.

If You See My Get Up And Go...
Tell Me Where It Went!

You know those types of days. You have a nagging cold that isn't bad enough to keep you in bed, but it's sure terrible enough to make you feel like you stuffed your head in a goldfish bowl.

The kids all look distorted, their jabbering is muffled and punctuated by 'clinks' as they tap on the bowl...and there's this drippy thing right between your eyes...no, not the goldfish, your nose.

How can a mother get anything done when she's got a runny nose? Add to that a few sneezes and we're talking about a real challenge! Have YOU ever tried to change a diaper with a head cold?

Oh, sure the naïve masses think, "So what's the problem? You can't smell anything."

No, but you can give your baby a heart attack. While you are trying to grab both legs so the baby doesn't dance in his diaper (they can do that, you know, without ever getting up off their backs) you're busy wiping your nose with one tissue and wiping his derriere with another. You're alert enough not to mix up what tissue goes where, and you're snuffling so you can get the diaper under the baby just so without dripping all over the place, when, wham—"ACHOOOOO!!!"

You could send a baby into convulsions doing that.

But, lucky you. Once you get the kid's eyeballs back in their sockets, he's decided it was actually fun and now busts into a hearty gut-laughter every time you sneeze.

Just in time for the kids who are now arriving home from school. Into the house they bound and see mom still wearing her robe, her hair is a tangled mess, her eyes are bloodshot with dark circles, her nose is brighter than Santa's lead reindeer, she's leaning against the wall for support, snuffing and then, "ACHOOO!!!" And what do the kids say?

"Mom, what's for snack?!"

KERPLUNK.

The kids prod your body with the toes of their sneakers but all you can do is moan and thank God for the cool tile floor against your cheek.

Later your husband arrives home. He's much more observant than the children who are running around the house in loincloths and waving spears over their heads. The first thing he wants to know is how you got footprints all over your back. When he rolls you over, he gasps. You're not the lovely woman he married!

But even though you couldn't swat away a gnat to save your life, you make a mental note to clobber him for grimacing and looking so startled. It's not like HE'S always in prime form.

Then, there are the magic words, ringing in your ears and slowly echoing away into peaceful oblivion because the cold tablets are finally kicking in. Your husband cradles your head in his lap and pats your cheek. "Honey?"

You stare back up at him, blinking in awe.

He holds your face between his hands and stares deeply into your eyes to make sure you are conscious enough to hear: "What's for dinner?"

Weight Games

I went outside to let the dog relieve himself on the lawn and my dear husband walked out right behind me, locking the door, and off he went to work leaving me stuck outside while my two-year old and three-year old were inside. Of course they REALIZED that they were out of mom's reach and they proceeded to get into everything they know is off limits.

So I tried to break into my own house and the only window that opened was the slim bathroom window, five feet off the ground and about six inches wide (which is less than HALF my girth).

I propped up a chair and got my leg in, then tried to SQUEEZE 190 pounds through that opening and half way through I got quite stuck, my legs dangling and helpless, and visions of Pooh Bear stuck in Rabbit's hole came to mind along with the fear someone would have to

166

call the local volunteer fire department to get me out. Talk about a wedgie.

I made a last desperate attempt to force my derriere through the window and lunged letting gravity s-l-o-w-l-y pull the rest of my carcass through and at last I was in the house, bruised but in!

Shouldn't this inspire me to lose the 60 pounds I need to lose? You'd think it would!

But, like most people, when confronted with my weight, as much as I want to lose the pounds, I'm probably not going to do anything very serious about it until I have a major scare. Like if they announce that there is a worldwide shortage on cheesecake!

Meanwhile, I play games with myself. TOMORROW, I will start anew. Today I will eat just one more cookie and just one more piece of chocolate. Oops, that was an odd number. I need to eat one more piece to make it an even number of bites. Oops, that leaves half of a candy bar. I better eat the other half to really make it equal.

THEN, I need to eat one more cookie because I feel guilty that I ate more than I'd originally planned to eat. Oh, well, now I might as well just wait until TOMORROW to start anew because I've blown it for today.

Do you know what I'm talking about? How come we don't do that with exercise? Hmmm, I just walked three blocks; I better walk one more just to make it even. Oops, that's five, just one more to make it six.

I read somewhere that if you sniff vanilla extract it will eliminate the desire for chocolate or some sort of calorie laden baked goodie and fool your brain into thinking you've satisfied the craving.

I don't know about you, but when I want to EAT something, the last thing I think about is sniffing extract and, knowing me, once I opened the bottle I'd start thinking of my favorite cookie recipe.

So tomorrow I will start anew—again. Just as soon as I whip up this batch of cookies and eat just a small equal portion....

Exercising With Toddlers

I've been exercising (okay it's only been twice—but I DID it!) to some of Richard Simmons' exercise videos.

Let me tell you. I thought I had it all worked out. I'd wait until anyone old enough to laugh at me had gone to school or work for the day, but noooooooooo. Were all my problems solved by that little strategy? Not on your life!

At first the toddlers happily plunked themselves on the sofa. I guess they thought we were going to watch a new movie.

Then the action started and they looked agog, then bewildered by my strange movements. What in the world is mom DOING?????

And then they started throwing obstacles in my path—sofa cushions, toys, the remote (as if to say, "Change the channel!") They even attacked my legs and tried to hold me still.

So being the devoted mom that I am…I put them in their room to play with a billion toys so I could do this little thing for myself for thirty minutes. Oh, the protests and the wails! What a terrible mom I am!

But I jiggled on, ignoring their pitiful cries and even ignoring the phone. And when I was done, I'd successfully sweat buckets and had the old heart pumping nicely.

The next day I tried again. Immediately, the kids cried out when they saw the little man with the puffy 'do.' He was NOT as motivating to my toddlers as he apparently was to the group exercising with him. My two-year old quickly turned off the television.

I turned it back on.

"Spob," I was told, which translates to SpongeBob.

"No Spob. Momma needs to exercise."

So the other grabbed the remote and managed to change the channel to The Wiggles. And then THEY started dancing around in front of the television. "Move over, Mom. This is how it's done!"

Yet again another mom in the universe is dated by her choice in music, or in this case exercise program. Gee, I bet Richard Simmons never thought of his exercise routine in that fashion. Next to The Wiggles, who can really work up a sweat of their own, Richard himself is an oldie.

So much for the video, Mr. Simmons! Today we're going to point our fingers and do the twist. Then, we're gonna go up and back down get back up and turn around. Can you point your fingers and do the twist?

Yes, I can! Apparently, if Momma wants to exercise while the Wiggles play, then she can exercise all she wants!

So now the toddlers and I are in sync. And it's working into our daily routine pretty well. I'd write more, but I have to 'do the monkey, elephant and tiger,' right after I dance with hot potatoes, mashed bananas and cold spaghetti.

Exercise? Me?

I was visiting an online community and the discussion was exercise. Now I'm a big fan of exercise. I love a good work out. That's why I make lots of lemonade. It gets hot sitting in the sun watching other people power-walk past my house.

One person posted a challenge to inspire us to exercise:

> Level 1 – 60 min.
> Level 2 – 90 min.
> Level 3 – 120 min. and so on.

I asked, "What's this?? 60 minutes a day, week, month or YEAR? I'm clearly in the 'year' category."

"Lisa, you crack me up!"

"Yeah, but I'm SERIOUS. I parked my butt six years ago and I haven't taken it out for a drive since…which probably explains the extra sixty pounds I am carrying in the trunk."

Isn't it the truth? Somewhere you go from being a child on-the-go to a sedentary adult. If you haven't, don't tell me. I couldn't handle the truth.

So I went on a 'diet' for the first four days of July. I tried an all fruit and veggie diet. Man, did that make me grouchy. Why can't I just WILL this extra weight off like I did when I was younger?

Then I thought, who wants a skinny grandma, anyway? I'm going to be a grandma someday so I'm just getting in shape for it now. My friend agreed. What will the grandkids want to hear? "Anyone for carrot sticks?" or "Brownieeeeeeees!"

Another friend said she went on a bike ride and thought her heart would pop out of her chest. I could sympathize. Just thinking about exercise makes my heart beat that hard.

Why is it that when you cut out the junk food and eat right you GAIN weight? I went up four pounds during my diet stint. Then, I went back to my normal grazing and dropped back down. What can we conclude from this? Cortisol is responsible.

Cortisol is the hormone that is released under stress. You go on a diet, you miss your favorite foods, you stress over this, you release cortisol and then you gain weight. You can't win!

The truth is that I am getting sick of walking into the wind and looking like I'm nine-months pregnant. The gossip-news is carrying on about how it looks as if Brittney Spears is having twins. Come on, I'm BIGGER than Brittney Spears!

My mom suggested a girdle. I've seen the ads. A girdle can make you look svelte and pounds lighter. But is it worth the mad hornet I'd turn into squeezing into one? How about those stretchy things that start from just under your breastbone and go down to just above your knees? I could make PMS history wearing one of those things.

"And here is a memorial to a woman all of us can aspire to. She took out three parking meters and a pedestrian's purse the day she tried wearing one of those cruel spandex body-suits…in the middle of summer…in a van without air-conditioning."

I am committed to getting back in shape. I'd like to be a healthy forty-year old. That means I've got to start walking. And I have. Today I walked from the computer desk to the refrigerator. This afternoon I'm going to walk from the front door to the van. As a bonus I might walk from the van to the mailbox…just as soon as I pull up alongside the curb. Hey, small steps!

Five Pounds of Chocolate Converts To...
WHAT!?!?!

Does it make sense to you that five little pounds of chocolate can equal twenty pounds on the scale? I'd like to know how that's possible.

But that's not the real reason I have a few pounds to lose. Medication for bipolar disorder and this wonderful thing called middle-age has my middle getting places a full twenty seconds before I do and it keeps on jiggling like a jogger waiting for the light to turn green at a four-way stop.

How embarrassing!

Now, I take great pride in knowing that my poor body has inherited its present shape largely due to the poundage of babies I have helped bring into this world, but there is nothing more frustrating than standing on that scale and seeing it mock me.

What do you mean I gained ANOTHER two pounds!?!?!

Does it matter?

For the longest time I have been trying to convince myself that the numbers on the scale don't matter as long as the clothes in my closet fit. Right?

Well, after a summer of shorts and loose T-shirts, I went to put on a pair of my 'fat' jeans and they don't fit!

Okay, I'm hitting the panic button here. Even the skirts I recently bought don't fit. Help!

It's time I hauled this carcass off the chair and out of the house and walked my you-know-what around the block a few times.

Sigh. Have you ever tried walking with a two-year old and a three-year old? The three-year old keeps moving closer and closer to the curb waiting for her little brother to bolt up someone's driveway so she can make a break for it across the street.

That ought to be enough exercise, right? It's enough to bust a sweat, that's for sure, but high blood-pressure doesn't equal weight loss it just makes me want to soothe myself with a nice piece of chocolate once I get back home and wonder what ever possessed me to try a stunt like that.

Oh, yeah. I need to lose weight.

How much? Sixty pounds now. Yikes!

Can you believe that I could run the 880 (1/2 mile) in 2 minutes and 42 seconds when I was 14 years old?

Nowadays I can sprint to the mailbox in the same amount of time. My mailbox is three houses away.

It takes me another two minutes to get my belly and butt to start jiggling in sync so I can ease them to a stand still. It's like watching one of those desk jobbies people have to amuse themselves (or annoy others) when they should be working, you know where the balls swing back and forth knocking each other? That's my front and backside. Swooop-pop-wiggle-jiggle-wiggle-jiggle.

I was always a skinny kid. This is like getting a "D" when you've been a straight-A student all your life.

Oh, well. What does that matter now? It's a new body and a new challenge.

This new week coming up I'll be working on 'moving my body more'.

I hate the word 'exercise'. It conjures up the image of the first of many P.E. teachers I had—a five foot Nazi, who stood there in her nice warm sweats and winter coat while we sprinted around the track it this hilarious one piece blue jump suit running, not because she'd sic the Dobermans on us, but because we didn't want to lose another finger or toe to frostbite.

Hey, whose idea was that to make kids on the verge of the EXTREMELY self-conscious teens dress like goons? We looked like a bunch of Smurfs running around with Gargamel over there yelling: "RUN ANOTHER LAP!!! RUN ANOTHER LAP, YOU STOOPID

SMURFS!!!"

Yeah, THAT will raise your self-esteem. NOT!

Well, the first of a new month is looming as large as my fanny. It's the day of the Great Weigh-In.

I'll be back to milk my "journey to a slimmer me" for all it's worth. Hey, you've got to laugh sometimes or it's just not fun at all.

Momma Cow

Did I say that I'd post my weight at the beginning of this month?
You BELIEVED ME??

HAHAHAHAHAHAHAHAHA.

It WAS 177. Apparently, two days later it was 182. I give up. I don't like the scale. I never did.

And NOW, I don't like my jeans either, but I need to rethink my position and get on speaking terms with them again. As it is, I don't fit into them and something needs to be done especially since they are my MATERNITY pants!

So naturally, I'm sitting here giving my fingers a great workout as I type this and sit on my bottom.

But I'm not here to complain. (You believe that, too???)

I was sitting and writing the other day when my two-year old toddled by. Now he's pretty verbose and has been stringing words together left and right. SpongeBob ball. Bottle nigh-night. Up dinner. Stuff like that. And those two-word sentences easily translate into more sophisticated sentences jam packed with meaning.

For instance, "SpongeBob ball?" means, "Where is the new ball my sister got for her birthday?" "Bottle nigh-night," means, "I'm tired and ready to go to bed, Momma." "Up dinner," means, "Please, put me up in my highchair so I can eat."

So just what do you think "Momma Cow" means?

Oh, I know what it means, all right. It means, "Momma is a big fat cow who sits around on her big fat butt all day and does nothing to work off those excess calories and stimulate that slowing middle-age metabolism of hers and she's using medication as an excuse for her weight gain but we all know it comes down to a matter of having the correct attitude and willpower because with proper daily exercise and an appropriate meal plan, Momma could slim down nicely, but no, she'd rather hide behind a big scoop of chocolate ice cream and add to her bathroom scale misery and poke fun at herself just to try to make other people laugh."

I told you my kids were bright. We don't even USE any expressions in our home with the word "COW" in it, so I'm thinking that this kiddo is AMAZING. Except, I don't like all the attention he's giving me.

Momma Cow.

Out of the mouths of babes.

This is what God gives me. This is the divine intervention I get when I asked God to help me lose some weight.

Just because I like to have dessert for breakfast doesn't mean I need a two-year old to tiptoe up behind me and say, "Momma Cow!" Or stroll casually through the living room while I am battling the temptation to steal a piece of chocolate from my dear husband's stash, and gibber with glee, "Momma Cow! Momma Cow!"

Who set him up to be the grand pooba super-conscience in this house, huh?

Well, I can tell you one thing. It's working!

But I am DEFINITELY keeping those cute baby pictures of him that are sure to embarrass when I share them with his fiancée in the future!!

Momma Cow my eye.

Moooooooooooooooooooooooo!

Burn Fat At Night

I actually got an email making that claim. I had to wonder if the sender had been reading my columns or not. For those who have read me long enough, you know that I have a love-hate relationship with my bathroom scale—just like every other woman on the planet—but I actually try to reason with the thing.

"Oh, come on! You mean one extra scoop of ice cream nets me two pounds? I drank all the water the experts say to drink! That's what it is, isn't it? You're weighing my water content, aren't you?"

No answer.

"Fine. Be that way."

I always MEAN to never speak with the scale again, but the next morning there it is mocking me with my three non-favorite numbers 1 – 8 – 7. Phooey.

Does your scale make weird sounds? Mine groans. And mumbles. No, it's not my husband—he's snoring away in the bedroom. It's definitely the scale making some smart remark about my binging after 7PM. "Who asked for your opinion?"

"You did."

Yes, it's time to lay off the ice cream sundaes before bed! The last thing I need is for my husband to haul me off to the mental ward because he overheard the scale speaking back to me.

So I contemplated the email. It was the typical SPAM: a big promise in the subject line with hardly enough content in the email to warrant opening it.

Still the thought stimulates my imagination. Wouldn't that be great? You go to bed a size 2X and you wake up a size 16. (Small steps here.) And every morning your husband and kids comment about the strange dreams they had. "I dreamed of roast beef!" "My dream was about popcorn…" "I thought somebody was frying bacon!"

And each morning the scale congratulates you for your triumphant eight-hour fat burning session.

That's the key to selling weight loss aids. Advertisements play up to our wishes no matter how unrealistic they may be.

- Burn fat while you sleep!

- Eat everything you want and the pounds just melt away!

- Never exercise again and look like Britney Spears!

- Lose weight eating all the junk food you like!

- Chocolate will make you live five years longer!

Yes, I sometimes succumb to the temptation and buy some of those magazines in the check-out line. You have to admit that the 'before' and 'after' pictures look really promising and there's not a hint of digital touching up. Even though you have a picture of a woman claiming to have lost 200 pounds by eating only birthday cake juxtapose a picture of the Pope being pelted by rocks from outer space, there's a part of you that wants to believe that it *could* be true!

Okay, maybe they were wrong about the celestial meteor shower – that wouldn't really happen. There's the Pope-mobile after all. But it is possible to lose significant amounts of weight by eating birthday cake alone. There has to be. It's probably some strange chemistry between the cake and the frosting that burns fat when the moon is full and perfectly aligned with Venus.

So the other night, my husband gently called my diet to my attention. I was stuffing cake in my mouth by the light of the refrigerator. He didn't even have the decency to shuffle in his slippers to prepare me for his arrival. With whipped cream on my nose, I met his rueful stare.

"What??? It's a full moon!"

Strong Like A Woman

I don't know where people got the impression that women were the weaker sex, especially when you consider that many women today (as always) gestate, carry around a living, developing baby, go through intense labor, give birth and the next day they are nursing a baby while they vacuum, make grocery lists, chaperone toddlers, negotiate with their teenagers and order meat for the freezer all while standing over a hot stove cooking dinner.

And there are those who wonder why women go insane roughly every 24 to 30 days a month.

If we didn't have this biologically programmed vent every month, we'd explode. It keeps us sane, while it drives everyone else insane.

Chocolate is our mainstay. We happily consume it by the pound one week, then lament it the next when we retain every body of water within a three hundred mile radius.

Women have known for years what scientists seem to have only discovered lately. Chocolate makes women happy. So does ice cream. Make that chocolate ice cream and nearly half the women in the world will be putty in your hands.

And if you believe that, you must be one of the men who think there is a method to our madness. There isn't. Bug off.

Would you like a back massage?

It gets that way, doesn't it ladies? We didn't ask to be simultaneously affectionate, hostile, ecstatic and tearful at the turn of a calendar page. Who in their right mind would?

That's like asking for bipolar disorder. I ought to know. I've got the disorder myself. Think PMS to the 100th degree and that's me on a good day without my medication. Kind of makes you want to invest in some top home security and stop toying with the idea of building that bomb shelter, doesn't it?

Don't worry. I like you. Today. At this moment.

WHAT ARE YOU STARING AT?!

They say that when women are together in a group for a long space of time, they synchronize their periods. No kidding. This may be the key behind the philosophy that women should stay out of politics; stay out of a man's world.

Can you imagine how countries would be run if women the world over were in charge AND in sync?

186

Every twenty-four to thirty days people would run for their bomb shelters as war breaks out around the globe...followed shortly by many tearful peace treaties and hugs. A relative calm would settle over the duly humbled masses as their public servants happily worked together affirming one another, edifying each other's policies and cheering each other on.

But then, a change. It would start slowly with the turning of mirrors to the wall so that no figures could be reflected in them. Accusations would start to fly, loyalties would be questioned and every vending machine would be devoid of chocolate, signaling - you guessed it - a mass movement toward bomb shelters everywhere.

I know. Not nice. Women have made it so far. How can I make fun of us?

Lighten up. It makes the ride a lot smoother than it would otherwise be. That which doesn't kill us makes us stronger.

You just know it was a woman nursing a baby while vacuuming, making grocery lists, chaperoning toddlers, negotiating with her teenagers and ordering meat for the freezer all while standing over a hot stove cooking dinner that coined that phrase.

Conclusion

Just Because Your Kids Drive You Insane...
Doesn't Mean You Are A Bad Parent!

Every little thing is setting me off today: the little eight-year old, the little three-year old and the little two-year old.

Anybody want to rent a kid?

I know, I know. New parents and couples without children, especially those having a difficult time conceiving, say, "How can you even *say* a thing like that?"

May you be blessed abundantly and soon know the answer for yourself personally!

It isn't that parents don't appreciate their children. It's that we are overwhelmed by how much there is to appreciate.

Like having a child dancing in place, screaming because the cup of milk wasn't placed just so next to three, count them, exactly THREE cookies. This would be the blessing of a two-year old.

How about the wail of a child who cannot possess every item she sees? "MINE, MINE, MINE, MINE, MINE!" "No, you can NOT have these scissors/this newspaper/my soda/your brother's favorite truck/the tax returns!"

Or a child running through the fifth lie in a row to explain the shortage of candy in the candy box. "Um, ah, um, well, it's like, um…I don't know!"

Lies, talking back, whining, tattletales, dancing in place, holding their breath…this is why having pets is NOT like having children.

I've never seen a dog roll his eyes and huff when you tell him to pick up after himself, as if he *could*. I've never had a cat smart-mouth me. Dogs don't hold their breath when you refuse them a treat before dinner. Cats don't follow you around informing you of every misdeed that the other pets committed.

In fact, dogs and cats stay cute. Kids outgrow it. Before you know it, that wonderful new baby scent is gone and it's no longer a novelty to drive them around town and show them off. Now it's just a chore. And no matter how many deodorizers you hang on their nose, that new baby smell never quite returns.

No, God has a great sense of humor. He decided to bless them with odor and as a parent you will become an expert at identifying these odors because if the kids don't stink in some fashion, their rooms, backpacks, lunch bags and car seats will.

Parents start out as reasonable and rational human beings. But over the years, all that gradually erodes. No matter how many parenting guides we read in the beginning, no matter ho many pre-natal classes we took, no matter how we prepped our tots for pre-school and kindergarten, we slowly turn into a shifty-eyed adult with a nervous facial tic…because we are always in a state of wonder.

"Why me?" "Why now?" "Why, God, why!?"

We're shifty-eyed because we're always looking for the cause of our steadily increasing dementia. Where is that spouse that suggested that having kids was a wonderful thing that would enhance our relationship? Whenever the kids start, we ask them, "Where's your mother/father?" as if our spouse has any answers.

We've got facial tics because we can't even sneak down the hall to isolate ourselves in the bathroom without some little one following us. "Where are you going? What are you doing? Can I come, too?"

We're turning into old people fast. And there's nothing we can do about it. It's *them!* They are sucking the life from us!

How else do you explain morphing from a calm, rational adult into a hunched over, suspicious, crooked-finger-pointing parent? We've *become our parents!* The curse is worse than we thought it would be!

So just because your kids drive you nuts sometimes doesn't mean you're a bad parent. It very well could mean you're an INVOLVED parent—a scar-bearing member of the Parent Corps—and your greatest ally is a good sense of humor as well as the ability to laugh at and make light of the challenges of parenting.

Suddenly, the noise of the kids swells and the sound is quickly followed by a loud crash accompanied by running tattlers all pointing their fingers at one another. All is as it should be.

Now where is that husband of mine...?

About The Author

Lisa has a bachelor's degree in creative writing from San Francisco State University. Her writing career includes articles for agricultural magazines, radio and television ads, copy for print ads and websites and a successful one-year stint in 2002 as a monthly community columnist for The Salinas Californian.

Returning as a self-syndicated columnist in 2004 armed with enough anecdotes about REAL life as a parent-in-the-trenches (and following the ONLY rule a creative writer should ever follow: write what you know), Lisa created Jelly Mom™, a parenting humor column, to help 'preserve' her sanity and that of others.

You can read (and subscribe) to the Jelly Mom™ column at www.jellymom.com as well as find it on many parenting and humor websites and in newsletters, e-zines and a growing number of newspapers.

Jelly Mom™ is written by Lisa Barker and syndicated through Martin-Ola Press/Parent To Parent and is available for publication electronically and in print. For more information and details, please contact editor@parenttoparent.com or you can contact Lisa directly: LisaBarker@jellymom.com.

Lisa lives with her husband and five children in Greenfield, California. This is her first book.